Savannah

Folklore

Nicole Carlson Easley

Schiffer
Publishing Ltd

4880 Lower Valley Road, Atglen, Pennsylvania 19310

Other Schiffer Books on Related Subjects:
Savannah Architectural Tours Jonathan Stalcup.
  ISBN: 978-0-7643-2907-4 $14.95
Savannah Squares: A Keepsake Tour of Gardens, Architecture and Monuments Robert J. Hill II.
  ISBN: 0-7643-2047-5 $9.95
Savannah Spectres Margaret Wayt Debolt.
  ISBN: 0-89865-201-4 $9.95

Schiffer Books are available at special discounts for bulk purchases for sales promotions or premiums. Special editions, including personalized covers, corporate imprints, and excerpts can be created in large quantities for special needs. For more information contact the publisher:

Schiffer Publishing Ltd.
4880 Lower Valley Road
Atglen, PA 19310
Phone: (610) 593-1777; Fax: (610) 593-2002
E-mail: Info@schifferbooks.com

For the largest selection of fine reference books on this and related subjects, please visit our web site at:

www.schifferbooks.com

We are always looking for people to write books on new and related subjects. If you have an idea for a book please contact us at proposals@schifferbooks.com.

This book may be purchased from the publisher. Include $5.00 for shipping. Please try your bookstore first. You may write for a free catalog.

Designed by Stephanie Daugherty
Type set in University/NewBskvll BT/Woodtype Ornaments 2
ISBN: 978-0-7643-3409-2
Printed in the United States of America

Dedication

To my mother, Diane E. Carlson, who always told me I was not afraid of anything, even when she could see the fear in my eyes.

Contents

Acknowledgments

This book would not have been possible without the help of the following people and organizations: Cheryl Anderson, Alyssa Brown, Diane Carlson, Henry Carlson, Nathan Carlson, Tammy Carlson, Karen Chavez, Ruthanne Divine, Isabel "Izzy" Easley, Jerry Easley, Joel Easley, Mary Ellen Easley, Roman Easley, Megan Fordham, Mango Fordham, Heather Fuselier, Robert Fuselier, Rex Fuselier, Arminpa Hairston, Captain Judy Helmey, S. Denise Hill, Dr. Courtney Houston, Donald R. Holland, Garnie Holmes, Amber Jones, Richard Kack, Lance Mackey II, Barry Moline, Dr. Barbara Allison Simpson, Brenda Thompson, Sue Utley, Amy Zubaly, Anna Williams, Anne Williams, Allison Williams, Shannon Williams, Jake Williams, Karen Wortham, the Georgia Historical Society, Old Towne Savannah Tours, Old Savannah Ghost Tours, Oglethorpe Tours, Oglethorpe Inn and Suites, Mercer House Museum, Miss Judy Charters, The First African Baptist Church, The Pirates' House, The River Street Inn, Sixth Sense Savannah, The Smiling Pup, the Sorrel Weed House, and Savannah Walks.

Introduction

The city of Savannah, despite its reputation of prosperity and culture, is a melting pot of folklore, weird traditions and even stranger history. When I began writing Savannah Folklore, I thought I knew all of Savannah's secrets and at least most of its history. It's true that Savannah has come a long way from the days when General James Edward Oglethorpe laid out its first four squares. It fought with a fledgling United States for independence from Great Britain. It fought and lost what some still refer to as "the war of Northern aggression." As a colony, it even fought and disgraced its own founder for the freedom to enjoy liquor. Savannah has seen yellow fever plagues, devastating fire and the ravages of time.

But despite its history of war and death, it remains one of the most beautiful and visited cities in the United States. Even among the South, Savannah is known as a city of great hospitality. It is one of a handful of cities that General William Tecumseh Sherman spared on his rampage of destruction through the Southern United States, deciding instead to offer the city as a Christmas gift to President Abraham Lincoln. And, it is one of the few places that seems to celebrate its debauchery along with its refined culture.

The truth is that Savannah has always been a little bit different. Even in the early days of its founding the city seemed to easily burst forth from the constraints of puritan ideals, bucking against the dreams of its own founder who envisioned a place where everyone came from the same background, held the same religious beliefs, and refused the pleasure of libations for a life of hard work and Christian ideals. Savannah's residents embrace their differences, enjoy their city's natural seclusion, and celebrate the preservation of their history and their folklore on every square.

History and Folklore of Savannah's 24 Squares

Savannah's 24 squares are the heart of the city. They each have a unique history and folklore, from those that were established by Oglethorpe to those developed as the city grew and thrived, and those that were lost in the name of progress. The city's first four squares were Johnson, Wright, Ellis, and Telfair.

Johnson Square

Johnson Square was the first square laid out by General Oglethorpe when he arrived to build his colony. Oglethorpe named the square after a friend of his, South Carolina Colonial Governor Robert Johnson. The square is surrounded by Savannah's first place of worship, Christ Church. Revolutionary War hero General Nathaniel Greene is buried in the square beneath an obelisk. The square also features two fountains the foundations of which once served as public ovens for Savannah's earliest colonists. The square also features a sundial that is often run into by zealous and impaired drivers.

One of two fountains in Johnson Square. Its foundation once served as a public oven for Savannah's first colonists.

Wright Square

Wright, Percival, or Courthouse Square was Savannah's second square. Established in 1733, the square was originally named Percival Square for John Lord Viscount Percival, Earl of Egmont, and president of the Trustees of the Georgia colony. Although it was often called Courthouse Square because it was the location of the old and new courthouses, the square was renamed Wright Square in 1736 in honor of then Governor of Georgia James Wright.

Wright Square is also the burial site of Tomo Chi Chi, a leader of the Creek Nation of Native Americans and a close friend of General Oglethorpe. The square was the site of the colonists' courthouse and the location where colonial justice was meted out.

Ellis Square

Ellis Square, or Marketplace Square, was named for Henry Ellis, the second royal governor of the Georgia colony. Through the 1730s, the square was often called Marketplace Square because it served as a center for commerce, with four market houses, buildings with a marketplace on the first floor and areas for public functions on the second floor. Prior to 1864, slaves were traded in the square. In 1954, the square was demolished and a parking garage was constructed on the site. The city is currently working to restore the square. [39,40]

Telfair Square

Telfair Square, or St. James Square, was originally named St. James Square after a green space in the center of London. In 1883, it was renamed Telfair Square in honor of the Telfair family. The Telfairs include former Governor Edward Telfair and his wife, Sarah Gibbons-Telfair; their son, Congressman Thomas Telfair; and their daughter, Mary Telfair, the benefactor of Savannah's Telfair Museum of Art. The Telfair's family home, now The Telfair Museum of Art, is still located on the square.

Reynolds Square

Reynolds Square, or Lower New Square, was laid out in 1734. Originally called simply Lower New Square, it received the formal name Reynolds Square in the 1750s for former governor of Georgia Captain John Reynolds.

Oglethorpe Square

Oglethorpe Square, or New Upper Square, was laid out in 1742. Originally called simply New Upper Square, it was later renamed in hour of the founder of the Savannah colony, James Edward Oglethorpe.

Washington Square

Washington Square was laid out in 1790 and was named for George Washington, who visited Savannah that year. The square was the site of the colonists' garden, which grew mulberry, hemp, and indigo.

Franklin Square

Franklin Square, or Water Tank Square, or Reservoir Square, was laid out in 1790. It was named for Benjamin Franklin, who served as an agent for the colony of Georgia from 1768 to 1778. The square was originally known as Water Tank Square, or Reservoir Square, because it was the location of the city's water supply. The First African Baptist Church is located on Franklin Square.

Warren Square

Warren Square was established in 1791 and named for General Joseph Warren, a Revolutionary War hero who was killed at the Battle of Bunker Hill. Warren served as President of the Provincial Government of Massachusetts. During the Battle of Bunker Hill, Savannah residents sent Bostonians gunpowder that they had recently seized from the British. Returning the favor, Bostonians send shiploads of provisions to Savannah shortly after the city surrendered to General Sherman during the Civil War.

Columbia Square

Columbia Square was established in 1799. It was named Columbia, a combination of Christopher Columbus and Amerigo Vespucci. The square is home to the Isaiah Davenport House that legend claims was saved from demolition by seven ladies from the Historic Savannah Foundation who stood in front of the home refusing to let the wrecking ball take it down.

The Kehoe House, built in 1892 by an iron magnate, is also on Columbia Square. The outside window casings, columns, and ornamentation are made from iron.

Greene Square

Greene Square was established in 1799. It was named for General Nathaniel Greene, who was a Revolutionary War hero and an aide to General George Washington. Greene commanded southern forces during the Revolution. For his efforts, he was awarded Mulberry Plantation. A native of Rhode Island, Greene found southern heat and humidity difficult to bear. He collapsed at Mulberry Plantation and died of heat stroke.

The second African Baptist Church is located on the square. According to legend, General Sherman read "ten acres and a mule," an article that promised to free the slaves, from this

The Kehoe House, built in 1892 by an iron magnate, sits on Columbia Square. The outside window casings, columns, and ornamentation are all made of iron.

square. Later, Dr. Martin Luther King practiced his "I Have A Dream" speech in the square.

Chippewa Square

Chippewa Square was laid out in 1815 in honor of American soldiers killed in the Battle of Chippewa during the War of 1812. The square features a bronze sculpture of the founder of the colony of Savannah, General Oglethorpe, whose likeness faces south, with his sword drawn toward his one-time enemy, Spanish Florida.

Orleans Square

Orleans Square was established in 1815 and was named for General Andrew Jackson's victory in the Battle of New Orleans that took place that year. The square features a memorial fountain in honor of Savannah's early German immigrants.

Lafayette Square

Lafayette Square was laid out in 1837. It was named for Marquis de La Fayette, the French hero of the American Revolution, who visited Savannah in 1825. The square features a fountain donated by the Colonial Dames of Georgia that commemorates the 250-year anniversary of the founding of the colony. The Andrew Low House and the Hamilton Turner Inn are located on the square.

Pulaski Square

Pulaski Square was established in 1837 and was named for Polish General Casimir Pulaski, who died during the Siege of Savannah.

Madison Square

Madison Square was laid out in 1837 and was named in honor of James Madison, the fourth president of the United States. The square features a memorial to Sgt. William Jasper, a soldier who was mortally wounded during the Siege of Savannah. It is the location of the Green-Meldrim House, where General Sherman stayed during his time in Savannah.

Crawford Square

Crawford Square was established in 1841. It was named in honor of United States Secretary of the Treasury William Harris Crawford, who was born in Savannah in 1772. Crawford ran for the office of United States president in 1824, but came in third, losing to President John Quincy Adams and runner-up Andrew Jackson.

Chatham Square

Chatham Square was laid out in 1847 and was named for William Pitt, the First Earl of Chatham. Although he never visited Savannah, Pitt was known as a supporter of the colony.

Monterey Square

Monterey Square was established in 1847. It commemorates the 1846 Battle of Monterey, in which American forces under General Zachary Taylor captured the city of Monterey, Mexico, during the Mexican-American War. The square features a monument to Revolutionary War hero General Casimir Pulaski, who died during the Siege of Savannah. During a restoration project, human bones believed to be those of General Pulaski were found beneath the monument. [39,40]

The square is also the location of the Mercer House and the Congregation Mickve Israel, the third-oldest Jewish congregation in the United States.

Troup Square

Troup Square was laid out in 1851 and was named for former Georgia Governor, Congressman, and U. S. Senator George Troup. The square features a modern, iron sculpture of an armillary sphere supported by turtles. Savannah mayor Herman Myers originally donated a fountain resembling a dog in 1897 as a drinking fountain for Forsyth Park. It was moved to Troup Square later, and shortened to serve the canine citizens of Savannah. The Universal Unitarian Church is located on the square.

Calhoun Square

Calhoun Square, or Massie Square, was established in 1851. It was named for South Carolina statesman John C. Calhoun, who served as Secretary of War, Secretary of State, and as Vice President under John Quincy Adams and Andrew Jackson.

The square is sometimes referred to as Massie Square, after the nearby Massie neighborhood and school.

Whitefield Square

Whitefield Square was laid out in 1851 and was named for George Whitefield, an English clergyman and a friend of John Wesley, the founder of Methodism. Whitefield established a home for orphaned children that is still in existence. The square served as a burial ground for slaves after 1818, when backyard-burial of slaves was prohibited.

Elbert Square

Elbert Square was named for a Revolutionary soldier and governor of Georgia. It was later paved and the Chatham County Civic Center was built on top of it.

Liberty Square

Liberty Square was named after the Revolutionary War group The Sons of Liberty. Later it was paved and the current Chatham County Jail and Courthouse were built on top of it.

Savannah's Early History

1. One Man's Dream, A Country's Fortification

The settlement of Savannah was born in the 1700s. It was the dream and aspiration of Englishman James Edward Oglethorpe to found a place where Protestant Christians could practice their faith without fear. He envisioned a utopia where the poor of London could escape their suffering, people could share a belief in the same God, value hard work as healthy for the soul and community, and live together in peace and prosperity. It was a grand vision in stark contrast to the England of Oglethorpe's birth. There, syphilis-infected prostitutes roamed the streets and Christian Protestants and Jews were persecuted and punished for their beliefs because they were considered a threat to the community goal of "enforced unity of religion." The prevailing idea in London was that everyone in a community must hold the same religious beliefs and that those who strayed from those beliefs must be punished, to ensure that all the souls in the community would be saved. In Oglethorpe's London, those whose beliefs differed from the Roman Catholic Church were often forcefully removed from their homes and in the winter months left to die of cold or starvation.₁ Equally cruel and unreasonable, even for the time, debtors' prisons housed those who could not repay their debts. Anyone who was owed money could have a debtor imprisoned by the courts for lack of or late payment. And, although prisoners were held for the inability to pay their debts, they were expected to pay for their food and lodging within the prison. Some prisons provided food that was generally considered unfit for consumption. Death and disease were common, and many who had no resources were chained to the floor with spiked collars until they died of starvation.

According to popular belief, Oglethorpe's friend, Robert Castell, died in one such prison from a smallpox infection. That provided the inspiration for Oglethorpe to pursue his dream of a utopian settlement in Georgia. Oglethorpe envisioned a colony of Christian Protestants, with similar backgrounds and beliefs, living together in peace without persecution.

Savannah was not just a dream of Oglethorpe's. The British Parliament also envisioned the need for a Georgia colony, but for a much different reason. Parliament saw the immediate need for a British settlement as a buffer between its fledgling colonies in the Carolinas and the burgeoning Spanish settlements in St. Augustine. Oglethorpe's dream was exactly what Parliament needed. With the blessing of Parliament, Oglethorpe and his motley crew of clergy members, wealthy noblemen, common businessmen, and several lucky souls plucked from debtors' prisons arrived in what would be the settlement of Savannah on a cold, February day in 1733. These unlikely neighbors formed the first forty families of the 13th colony in the New World.

2. The Legend of Tomo Chi Chi

The weary travelers were greeted on the edge of the Savannah River by an imposing figure, a seven-foot tall, 80-year-old native with one good eye who stood stoically on the bank as they arrived. He was mottled with battle scars and wearing a cape of bearskin, signifying his membership in the Creek tribe. Tomo Chi Chi, leader of the nearby Creek village of Yamacraw, welcomed his visitors. [2]

Although it is doubtful that those aboard Oglethorpe's ship had ever set eyes on a native person before that day, many in the Creek tribe had been trading with white settlers in the Carolinas for many years. Tomo Chi Chi introduced Oglethorpe to a native woman by the name of Mary Musgrove. White settlers in the Carolinas had educated Musgrove and to Oglethorpe's surprise, she welcomed him in his native language.

Oglethorpe explained his plans to build his colony on the shores of the river. Tomo Chi Chi offered his blessing and led Oglethorpe to a bluff near the river highly suitable for the fledgling colony. Over the following weeks, settlers setup camp and Oglethorpe laid out the city. He began with four squares for homes and public buildings that surrounded rectangles of public land, a pattern he believed could be repeated to cover as much as five thousand acres of land.

In Oglethorpe's city, slavery and rum were prohibited because he believed both made men lazy, and hard work was good for the soul. Settlers toiled long hours to build their homes, plant crops, and secure their settlement in heat and humidity they could not have imagined. They found it difficult to work in the fields and were afraid of the alligators that walked casually down the dirt roads that connected their homes. Nearby swampland was a breeding ground for mosquitoes carrying the yellow fever disease. By the summer months, many colonists had fallen ill and the death rate was high. Oglethorpe's beloved colony was dying one settler at a time.

Then, a miracle arrived. A ship carrying several Jewish immigrants who had been trained in medicine came down the river. Although they did not fit the ideals of the settlement, Oglethorpe welcomed them and they tended to the ill, saving the colony. The experience opened Oglethorpe's mind to the idea that people of different faiths and cultures might be able to live together in peace. It wasn't long before other groups arrived in the colony seeking relief from persecution: Roman Catholics, Lutherans from Central Europe, Moravians from Bohemia, and men from the Highlands of Scotland all were welcomed to the Savannah settlement.

3. A Religious Utopia, as Long as There's Plenty of Rum

By 1742, Savannah had become a melting pot of people and cultures. Aside from the heat and hard work, colonists lived together in peace. But trouble eventually surfaced. Quiet grumblings about the prohibition of alcohol, anti-slavery ideals, and laws against women inheriting property were becoming louder and angrier as settlers heard stories of the prosperity some Carolina colonies enjoyed.

The success of Oglethorpe's colony was threatened as angry colonists left for an easier life in Carolina colonies. In 1749, a frustrated Oglethorpe bent his rules and allowed colonists to "borrow" slaves from the Carolinas, with the idea that the slaves would help his colonists for a short time and be sent back. The slaves built homes and other buildings and were sent back, as agreed, when the work was completed.

But damage had been done. The Savannah colonists had tasted a much easier life in the Carolinas and even more left to find it. Others began to quietly plot against their founder. Oglethorpe made two trips to England to recruit more settlers and request supplies for his colony. The disgruntled colonists used the circumstances to call for adjusting the rules of their colony. They created a pamphlet that detailed their belief that Oglethorpe was mismanaging the colony and causing its destruction. The pamphlet was sent to the British Parliament, and soon management of the Savannah colony was turned over to the King of England, George II. Oglethorpe was eventually cleared of wrongdoing and mismanaging the colony, but he never returned to Savannah.

A City Built on Its Dead

S avannah has long been referred to as "a city built on its dead," or a necropolis. In a city as old and historic as Savannah, there is hardly an inch of land where a battle has not been waged, a duel has not been fought, someone has not succumbed to the ravages of yellow fever, complications of child birth, collapsed from the summer heat, been frozen in the winter elements from lack of shelter or burned to death in the kitchen fires that plagued 17th century homes. Natives buried their dead there; Revolutionary battles, colonial duels, and Civil War skirmishes were fought there; and yellow fever, typhoid, cholera, influenza, smallpox, and heat stroke ravaged settlers not accustomed to the heat and humidity of the colony.

4. Life and Death in the Colony

Mortality records of the 17th century show that a great many people buried in the cemetery were women and children. Families were large and women married young, having children immediately. According to historical records, many women birthed a child once every year and a half. [3]

Women died from childbirth complications and lack of antiseptic. Even if the mother and child lived through childbirth, doctors delivered babies with dirty, ungloved hands. Many infants did not survive past the second year of life.

Drowning was one of the most common causes of death among Savannah colonists; most did not know how to swim. Others died from mortification (gangrene), delirium, consumption, tuberculosis, and inflammation of the bowels (appendicitis). Because death played such a large role in the life of the colony, one of its most challenging aspect was where to put the accumulating bodies. ₃

5. They Moved the Headstones

There are many cemeteries and less formal burial grounds throughout Savannah. Communities and houses of worship planned some, while others were sacred resting grounds for the natives. Among graveyards now lying beneath beautifully restored antique homes and modern streets is the burial ground of about a thousand slaves.

In 1791, the land where Calhoun Street sits was the outermost edge of town. It sat stark and empty just outside the walled city and became a popular burial ground for those people who were not members of the Church of England. As with many of the early burial grounds of the city, estates and the rambling mansions of the wealthy covered this graveyard during the cotton boom of the early 1900s.

Wright Square's homes and buildings are above Savannah's earliest formal graveyard. The first official colonial graveyard was established in 1733 with the burial of William Cos. Cos was the settlement's only surgeon and the first colonist to die in Savannah, purportedly from "bad Indian rum." Wright Square was originally called Percival Square after John Lord Viscount Percival, Earl of Egmont, and president of the trustees of the Georgia colony. It was also known as Courthouse Square, because it was the site of the settlement's first courthouse and, not unrelated, old "Convenience," "Justice" or "Lynching" Square for its grim history.[4.] In the 1800s, the square served the colony as a bastion of colonial justice with its courthouse, jail cells and hanging tree all within one convenient square. Those accused of crimes, such as stealing farm animals, swearing, inappropriate sexual relationships, public drunkenness, slander, and of course murder, would have their day in court knowing full well what awaited them in the square if things didn't go their way. Those who did not make their case often were dragged into the square for a public hanging from the square's oak tree and then dumped unceremoniously into the nearby graveyard to await burial.

Despite the bodies buried beneath their homes, or perhaps unaware of it, Savannah folks once were very concerned with the dangers of living too closely to their dead. Perhaps because of the waves of wretched fevers and illnesses that crippled the colonists often in the hottest months of summer or because superstitious and spiritual beliefs of African slaves had begun to mix with the settlers' mostly Episcopalian Christian religious structure, slaves told tales about lost and angry spirits, curses, shaman and the tools and rituals necessary to keep yourself safe from the dead who chose to stay and wander the earth to taunt the living.

Living in close proximity to the dead was considered unhealthy and unlucky. Colonists feared that decaying bodies might spread disease or that the disgruntled souls of the dead might wander their homes, or worse, take possession of their bodies. As Savannah grew, many burying grounds were excavated and bodies that could be moved were relocated farther from the city. Eventually, city planners became tired of digging up graves and reburying them. To pacify the public, they continued to move the burying grounds by moving the tombstones. They left the bodies where they were laid and built on the land over them. One of the most known examples of this is the original burying ground of the settlement of Savannah.

In the 1750s the city was growing. City officials decided to move the original Colonial Cemetery that lies beneath today's York, Bull, Oglethorpe, and Whitaker Streets to make room for the growing population. The burying grounds for the settlement of Savannah for seventeen years was set to be moved to a new cemetery to be built near Christ Episcopal Church. The project proved to be too expensive and time consuming, so officials compromised. They moved the head stones to the new cemetery and built the streets and buildings over the cemetery.

Of course, there are bodies buried throughout the city unconnected to any specific burial ground. In fact, the land where the modern-day city of Savannah sits has been collecting the dead for more than 400 years, even putting some to rest before they were ready. One of the most gruesome tales of Savannah's dead took place just after the American Revolutionary War.

In 1778, British troops maintained control of Savannah and American colonists were plotting to take it back. In 1779, they made their move with the help of French troops. On a cool October morning, French ships filled with French and American soldiers lined the Savannah coast. Soldiers slipped into the thick woods surrounding the colony with muskets and cannons. They hid in the deep protective trenches that surrounded the city. The Siege of Savannah began in the early morning hours with shots fired from a cannon and lasted for about two hours as more than 140 canons fired across the settlement.

When the last canon was fired, 1,000 people were dead, but only thirteen of them were British. The Americans and the

French had been outwitted and out warred and the men who had taken shelter in the trenches had taken the brunt of the canon fire. The British showed them no mercy. Even as they surrendered, the British continued their attacks eventually taking up shovels and covering the trenches filled with the French and American dead and wounded. Those who could not claw their way out were buried alive with their dead compatriots.[5]

By the early 1900s the people of Savannah had moved on from the Revolutionary War and were enjoying the prosperity of the cotton trade. Large ornate homes were built where trenches and watch towers once stood, exactly above the bodies of the men who fought and died to return Savannah to the American colonists. Today the Sorrel Weed House, the Green-Meldrim House and the Eliza Jewitt House stand above the trenches where soldiers of the Savannah Siege are haphazardly buried. In fact, occasionally their muskets, shell casings, and bones pop-up through aging basement floors or are uncovered during renovation projects.

6. Yellow Fever, The Mark of the Beast

The New "Old Colonial Cemetery" was built on the dirt roads of Abercorn, East Oglethorpe, and Habersham Streets and was enclosed with a wooden fence. It served the colonists for nearly 100 years. During times of relative health, with no outbreaks of disease spreading through the community, residents would hold wakes for their dead. The laying-out of the body was not only to give family members a chance to pay their final respects, but also an added measure to give the person presumed dead some time to wake up. Physicians of the time were mostly self-trained and often made errors when determining whether or not a person was dead. Many, in fact, did wake during their wakes. Unfortunately, others woke later.

After the wake, a horse-drawn carriage would carry the coffin to the Old Colonial Cemetery where it would be buried, unless the family owned a family crypt. The Old Colonial Cemetery is one of only a few cemeteries in the United States that has this particular type of underground family crypt. The crypts were built from a mixture of oyster shells, sand, and water and were sealed with a brick veneer.

Families who owned a crypt in the Old Colonial Cemetery typically designated one family member as the crypt keeper. It was the crypt keeper's job to visit the crypt every six months and remove current bodies from the shelves, dumping remains into an ash bucket to prepare for the next eternal resident. It was a stressful, lifelong position within the family, as crypt keepers occasionally had difficulty opening the crypt door because a body of a family member was huddled frozen against it, having been buried before their time.

During outbreaks of disease, city officials hired two men, called "bone collectors," to work the death wagon. Residents were instructed to stay inside their homes with the doors and windows closed tight. If there was a death in the house, you were to immediately throw the body on the front porch or stoop. The death wagon, pulled by a mule, came nightly to collect the bodies. Bone collectors would walk behind and throw bodies onto the wagon. The mule clopped along through the windy streets to the cemetery, where men threw the bodies into a mass grave and covered them with sand.

During the Revolutionary War, the fence around the Old Colonial Cemetery was damaged by musket and cannon fire. Residents became concerned that they might become ill, since packs of wild dogs and other scavenging animals had slipped through holes in the damaged fence at night to dig up bodies.

Animals often dragged bodies from the cemetery into today's Abercorn and Habersham Streets to feast and quarrel over the remains.

Citizens feared outbreaks of yellow fever, the "poisonous influenza," from living in close proximity to decomposing bodies. Savannah had again grown too close for comfort to the dead. A common belief of the time was that sickness seeped from infected bodies into the night air and breathing-in the early morning fog caused the fever. They treated the disease by drinking turpentine. To answer their fears, the city built a strong, 300,000-brick encasement that protects the cemetery today. The city's horse-drawn hearses accessed the cemetery through a brick path from the entrance at South Broad Street to the exit at Perry Lane.

In reality, the dreaded disease was carried by swarms of mosquitoes that lived and bred in swamp lands outside the city. Savannah suffered outbreaks of yellow fever in 1820, 1845, and 1870.

By the summer of 1820, bone collectors had collected and buried 700 bodies and deposited them into the mass grave in Old Colonial Park Cemetery. Legend stipulates the number of dead to have been 666, the number of "the beast" or devil from the prophetic Book of Revelations from the New Testament of the Bible:

> He ordered them to set up an image in honor of the beast who was wounded by the sword and yet lived. He was given power to give breath to the image of the first beast, so that it could speak and cause all who refused to worship the image to be killed.
>
> He also forced everyone, small and great, rich and poor, free and slave, to receive a mark on his right hand or on his forehead. No one could buy or sell unless he had the mark, which was the name of the beast or the number of his name.

In this cemetery many victims of the Great Yellow Fever Epidemic of 1820 were buried.

Nearly 700 Savannahians died that year, including two local physicians who lost their lives caring for the stricken.

Several epidemics followed. In 1854 The Savannah Benevolent Association was organized to aid the families of the fever victims.

According to historical records, by the summer of 1820, the bone collectors had collected and buried hundreds of bodies and deposited them in the mass grave in Colonial Park Cemetery. The actual number of dead was 666, the same number as the mark of the beast or the devil from the prophetic Book of Revelations from the New Testament of the Bible. Church leaders who were uncomfortable with the death count changed the number of the dead from 666 to "nearly 700," and that is the number that is engraved on the cemetery's historical marker.

> This calls for wisdom. If anyone has insight, let him calculate the number of the beast, for it is man's number.
> His number is 666.[6]

Church leaders were uncomfortable with the final death count. They changed the number of dead from 666 to nearly 700 in their records. That is the number that is engraved on the Yellow Fever historical marker of the Old Colonial Cemetery.

In 1846, the city of Savannah added trees and shrubs around the grounds of the cemetery for added protection from impurities. Fevers worsened and fear about what toxins might be seeping from the Old Colonial Cemetery continued. In 1849, the city government established a new burial ground outside the city limits. County health officials encouraged families to have their relatives' bodies removed from the Old Colonial Cemetery and re-buried at the newly established Evergreen Bonaventure Cemetery.

A collection of tombstones from the early and mid-1800s line the east wall of the Colonial Cemetery. The tombstones were removed in 1895 to make room for walkways and trash receptacles when the cemetery became a park.

The few graves and tombstones that remained in the Old Colonial Cemetery were left to fall into disrepair; many eventually crumbled and were forgotten, along with the bodies they marked. In 1895, the Old Colonial Cemetery became a city park.

Headstones were ripped from the ground to make way for walkways and trash receptacles. The graves and bodies encased within them were left where they lay. Park planners mounted uprooted tombstones against the brick ledge of the east wall of the cemetery where they remain today.

In 1913, the Daughters of the American Revolution constructed an archway at the northwest corner of the cemetery, which now serves as the main entrance. The bricked-in park includes about 60 headstones and more than 13,000 bodies.

Evergreen Bonaventure Cemetery has since become one of the most famous cemeteries in the United States. Its many grand and artistic tombstones almost compete with each other and the natural beauty of its land for visitors' attention. Its history and folklore surround the land and the dead who lie just beneath the surface. It has been described as a lush and beautiful "city of the dead," so enticing that some say visitors have thrown themselves into the nearby river so they never have to leave.[7]

The Cemetery, locals say, is a perfect example that evil can exist in the purist of places, and wickedness often thrives in great beauty. Bonaventure Cemetery folklore tells of a pack of wild ghost dogs that roam the cemetery grounds emitting heavy, labored breaths and low, deep growls. The phantom beasts have been known to chase visitors and threaten them with snarling lips and snapping jaws if they visit too long in the evening hours. Also among the folklore of the cemetery is the grave of a little girl named Gracie Watson. The life-size statue of

Evergreen Bonaventure Cemetery features beautiful sculptured gravestones. The Cemetery has been described as a "lush city of the dead."

In 1913, the Daughters of the American Revolution constructed the archway
to the Old Colonial Park Cemetery. The New "Old Colonial Cemetery" was
originally built on the dirt roads of Abercorn, East Oglethorpe and Habersham
streets encased within a wooden fence. It served the colonists of Savannah for
nearly a hundred years.

Gracie is said to cry out in the night, especially if toys
and gifts that cemetery visitors leave at her grave are
disturbed.

The Evergreen Bonaventure Cemetery also contains a most
hospitable place of rest, The Stranger's Tomb, that was originally
in the Old Colonial Cemetery. It contains an empty shelf and
offers those who pass away while visiting Savannah a place of
rest until their body can be moved to its final destination.

One of the most visited gravestones of the Evergreen Bonaventure Cemetery is a sculpture of little Gracie Watson. The life-size statue of the little girl is said to cry out in the night.

The Taming of the Dead

B ecause of prevalent disease and war, people in the early days of Savannah were acutely aware of their mortality. They acknowledged spirits of early settlers that they believed to roam their city, creep in and out of homes, wander the streets and cemeteries, and rest below their feet. Therefore, Savannah today is considered to be one of the most haunted cities in the United States. Among the many graves that lie beneath the city are those that once were marked by gravestones, bodies of people killed in battle, and those that were buried in unmarked graves intentionally for the protection of the dead and living alike.

7. The Journey to the Other Side

Savannah's early European settlers were thoroughly steeped in the culture of Christianity, but they lived and worked with second- and third-generation people who practiced indigenous African religions that were filled with rituals, superstitions, rites, and passages for the living as well as the dead. The colonial culture of Savannah became a mesh of Christian dogma and tribal African customs. This was especially evident when traditions meshed well, such as Christians teaching that the living should not communicate with the dead and

Africans helping the dead on their way to the next world and protecting the living from those who refused to move on. In tribal traditions practiced in Savannah, the living played an important role in defining space between the living and the dead, and that separation was secured through rituals. Many of the rituals are still practiced in Savannah today.[8]

When African Americans buried their dead in Savannah, the bodies were laid to rest in unmarked graves or were surrounded by fences with no gates, to protect the dead from visitors, so that they could make their journey to the next world in peace. Cemeteries were sacred places; once the dead were settled, they were not visited again. When a generation passed, so did information about where its dead were buried. Like other traditions of the dead around the world, these bodies were buried with items they would need on their journey:

> "a cup of water to quench their thirst; a jar of rice to quell their hunger; a lantern to light their way; a pistol carved from wood for protection; a bed frame for rest; and a collection of herbs to keep them healthy."[8]

Just as bodies of those who lived before had formed the foundation of the living in the city of Savannah, the recently dead and their needs in afterlife have grown into a culture and folklore of Savannah today. One of the most practiced rituals was the use of "haint blue" to protect the living from spirits who had not moved on because they were disturbed in their journey or had unfinished business with the living. Haint blue is a blue-green paint color that represents water. Because it was traditionally, and still is, mixed from whatever materials are available, it can range from a watery representation of green to deep blue. They believed the dead could not pass over natural elements such as water and blood.[8]

Shades of haint blue can be seen throughout Savannah. It coats the ceilings of churches and seals the entrances of homes, including doorways, porches, and windowsills. Inside, it coats rooms where women gave birth, to protect the newborns and laboring mothers.

Wealthy residents of Savannah built rooms in their homes with curved corners, so that sneaky spirits could not lurk in the corners. They believed rounded corners would send spirits through the house and right back out the front door. Drainage spouts in the shapes of Mahi Mahi fish donned many homes of the wealthy, protecting them from evil spirits.

Those who could not afford to round their rooms relied on other protections, such as "spirit trees." They were trees covered with colorful glass bottles that tinkled and clanked melodiously in a breeze. The bright colors and clicking glass attracted wandering spirits that became trapped within the swaying bottles.

It is not just those who believe in spiritual traditions of descendants of slaves who run into problems with angry spirits in Savannah. Many people, even today, turn to religious leaders to cleanse themselves and their homes with prayer, blessings, and exorcisms. Just as with the living, the dead of Savannah do not always play by the rules.

8. "Blessing" the House on St. Julian Street

There is a beautiful, crisp, white home on St. Julian Street with windows that reach out of its gamble roof toward the sky above and the street below, welcoming sunlight and shadows. It is a warm and welcoming home with a dark secret.

The House on St. Julian Street was "blessed" by a Bishop from the Episcopal Church during its restoration because its then owner, James Arthur "Jim" Williams, felt there was an evil presence in the home.

Built between 1796 and 1799, the house became the home of James Arthur "Jim" Williams, a well-known antiques dealer and historic home preservationist, in the 1980s. At the time, Savannah was in a state of disrepair and Williams was embroiled in a battle with developers who sought to rip up Savannah's squares and tear down its historic homes to build modern shopping centers and business offices, college classrooms, and dormitories.

The city of Savannah was being transformed from a village whose citizens lived and worked around its squares to a sprawl of modern concrete, metal, and glass. Crime was on the rise downtown and prostitutes wandered the squares; brothels and bars littered the historic district. Wealthy residents had mostly abandoned the historic downtown mansions in favor of new construction closer to shopping centers and offices. Homes on many of the squares were in disrepair and in danger of demolition. Williams sought to restore the beauty of Savannah by purchasing and refurbishing one dilapidated house after another.

The home on St. Julian Street was one of his projects. It was originally located on Hampton Lilly Bridge Road. As a part of the restoration process, Williams had it moved to St. Julian Street. As restoration efforts began, Williams and his workers found that progress did not go smoothly. Contractors struggled to move the home and a wall fell, killing one of the workers. Beneath the house they discovered a brick crypt that had been filled with water. They moved the home with the crypt still in its foundation, drained the water and filled the crypt with concrete. When the home was finally in place on St. Julian Street, inside and outside renovations began.

The mason who had been mortaring bricks outside the home reported continuously hearing someone walking and moving around in the house when he knew it was empty. Voices and the sounds of unsettled human and animal movement escaped from the windows and walls, as though the house itself were alive.

Workers inside the home heard the same strange noises that always seemed to be upstairs when they were working downstairs, and downstairs when they were working upstairs, or just in the next room. A worker who had just completed varnishing the upstairs floors and had begun work downstairs heard the sound of someone walking in an aimless pattern on the floors above. He knew there was no one up there.

When the refurbishing was complete, Williams moved into the home and celebrated his first night with a party. After the party, Williams went to bed satisfied with his home, but as he lay in bed he listened to sounds of someone or something walking in the home. It was the first of many sleepless nights for Williams. He described the feeling in the lower level of the house "like a mausoleum."

Williams never felt comfortable in the home. He told friends he could not shake the feeling that someone or something in the house wanted to hurt him. Sometimes he felt pressure tightening around his neck as though an unseen force was trying to choke him. At night, he lay in bed frozen with fear and listened to sounds of something walking in circles around his bed, a noise he described as sounding as though someone was walking on glass or oyster shells.

During a buying trip in Europe, Williams' neighbors called to tell him that a man was staying in his house. They could see him pacing the floors and peering angrily out of the windows. Distraught, and not excited about the idea of returning to his home, Williams called a Bishop from the Episcopal Church to bless the house and exorcise its demons.

The Bishop performed the rite of exorcism – walking from room to room clutching the bible and the cross as a symbol of the defeat of Satan through the death of Christ. He recited the prayer for Solemn Blessings of the Crucifix:

Ut quóties triúmphum divínae humnilitátis, quae supérbiam nostri hostis dejecit. Dignáre respícere, bene + dícere et Sancti + ficáre hanc creaturm incensi, ut omnes languores, omnesque imfirmitates, atque insidiar inimici, odorem ejus sentientes, efffugiant, et separatur a plasmate tuo; ut num quam lædatur amorsu antiqui serpentes Numquam lædatur a morsu antiqui derpentis.

(How often the divine humility has triumphed casting out the pride of our enemy. Deign to care for bless and sanctify those being inflamed by passion and weakness, any sickness, deceits of the foe and suspicious resentments felt by them. Be cast out and driven away from your creature. Never to be hurt by the bite of the ancient serpent.)[9]

When the "blessing" was complete, Williams returned, but the uneasy feeling and noise in the night continued. Williams became exasperate and called the Bishop about the failed exorcism, to which the Bishop replied, "I don't see how I can help you, your spirit is obviously not Episcopalian."

Williams decided the house had won the battle and continued to live in the home with the strange activities until he could sell it. Williams sold the home to a wealthy family with small children. The new residents did not report experiencing any feelings of dread, but they did become accustomed to the male voices that continued to whisper and flit about the home and the pacing footsteps that filled the quiet hours of the night. One evening, a guest visited them for dinner, but left abruptly because he said he felt as though something in the home wanted to hurt him. As he was leaving, he said he felt he was being choked.

9. The Exorcism of Lori Green

Nationally known spiritual leader and exorcist, Bob Larson, is the pastor of Spiritual Freedom Churches International, based in Phoenix, Arizona. He has also visited Savannah. Larson espouses the belief in, and benefits of, "integrative emotional healing and spiritual deliverance, for whole-person wellness," which in many cases includes exorcisms.

The Church offers a "Demon Test" to the public through their website, where one can discover whether or not they are possessed by demons and evil spirits by answering questions such as, "Are you sometimes overwhelmed with feelings of severe depression and hopelessness?" and "Do voices tell you to commit illegal acts, blaspheme God, or indulge in immoral acts?"

Larson has performed thousands of exorcisms throughout the United States and Europe, including the exorcism of Lori Green in the Sorrel Weed House of Savannah. As documented in the Sy Fy Channel show, "The Real Exorcist," in early 2008, Larson was called to Savannah to save Lori Green. Green, a mother of two young children, had become overwhelmed with thoughts of hurting and killing herself, thoughts she believed, and Larson agreed, came from evil spirits that had entered her body. Green confessed that she had played a part in her possession, having always had an interest in the occult. She felt drawn to haunted places. Green spent years reaching out to the dead, trying to communicate with evil spirits and welcoming them to enter her body and asking out loud for Jesus Christ to leave her body and her life.

The two met at the Sorrel Weed House, one of the most historic and some say, most haunted, homes in Savannah. Larson arrived at the Sorrel Weed House dressed in black. He carried with him his Bible, a large metal cross, and anointing oil. He met Green in the basement, a dark room with red brick walls and floors.

Green explained to Larson that, although she did not know when the spirits of the devil possessed her, she believed that several entities had taken possession of her body and that they were attempting to control her thoughts and actions. Green said at least one of the spirits had lived with her for years, becoming more and more pronounced in its demands. The voice of this evil entity had been telling her that she is worthless. It ordered her to cut her arms and legs until she bleeds. She contacted Larson, she said, "because now it wanted my life."

The Sorrel Weed House was built between 1839 and 1840. It was the site of the 2008 exorcism of Lori Green. The house is considered one of the most haunted properties in Savannah.

The demon, she said, was screaming in her head, demanding that she kill herself.

Larson sat across from her and stared into her face. With a look of quiet consternation, he began speaking to the evil spirits within her. He goaded the entities to "come out" and speak to him. After a short pause, Green emitted a deep growling voice, "she needs to be punished," it said. Larson shook the cross in front of Green's face and body.

Green's body began to mimic the movements of the cross, shaking and thrashing violently. She hit Larson repeatedly in his head and slapped the cross from his hands. Green continued to growl and moan as she thrashed.

Larson and his assistant grabbed her and held her still. It took both men's great effort to hold her down, as Larson continued the ritual. He grabbed Green's head, holding both of her ears tightly. He pushed his hands hard into her head as he yelled, "squeeze the demon out." Green became quiet and still.

Larson released her head and held her in an embrace for several moments. After the exorcism, Green confirmed that the evil entities were no longer inside her. She could not feel them or hear them. She left the Sorrel Weed House tired and calm, and, she said, "saved" from certain death.

Although there have been several exorcisms and blessings performed in Savannah throughout the years, there are many more people in the city who are completely comfortable living and working with the spirits that have taken permanent residence in their homes and grounds. In fact, there are hundreds of documented hauntings in the city of Savannah. They are boisterous poltergeists wreaking havoc in beautifully restored homes, slightly mischievous souls that re-arrange furniture and giggle, always just out of sight, and many more quiet, thoughtful spirits content to watch time pass through dark attic windows.

Hauntings in the City of Hospitality

According to the 2001 report of the American Institute of Parapsychology, the city of Savannah is one of the most actively haunted cities in the United States, with more reports of poltergeist activity than any other American city. Some say the extraordinary amount of haunting is due to the massive amounts of dead buried below its homes, businesses, and streets; others say it is the city's famous gray bricks, created by slaves from volcanic material culled from the bed of the Savannah River, that hold the people, actions, and emotions of the past in place like a battery. Most who have spent any time in the city agree: those who die here tend to stick around, some to work on unfinished business, some to protect the living, and others because they are simply still having fun.

10. The Sorrel Weed House

The Sorrel Weed House was the family home of Francis Sorrel, his wife Matilda Moxley, their many children, and several slaves. The family was well known in the city for throwing lavish parties that began in the home's front parlor and later spilled into the open space of Madison Square in the late evening hours. The 16,000-square-foot mansion has been the site of many murders, including the death of Matilda, and the lynching death of her close friend and slave, Molly.

The mansion and its carriage house function as a museum. Museum staff and visitors often see the shapes of people in the windows and reflected in the home's many mirrors–women in gowns and men wearing uniforms. A black mist in the shape of human forms wisps throughout the house and porches. Muffled female voices often are heard throughout the house, but especially in the front parlor. Visitors often report being tapped on the neck, the back of the head, and the shoulders. Several members of the staff and passersby have seen a woman dressed in a black, antebellum-style dress walking in front of the windows of the carriage house.

Before the house was a museum, a young man rented the apartment in the carriage house. Nightly, he heard a woman calling out for help. She often whispered his name. On one occasion, a tour guide was in the carriage house preparing the area for an upcoming tour. When he walked out of the building, a couple that had been standing on the street below approached him and asked if the lady in costume with him in the carriage house was part of the tour.

In 2008, the Transatlantic Paranormal Society (TAPS) of the Sy Fy Channel television show "Ghost Hunters" investigated the home. During the investigation, the image of a green hand appeared on the brick wall of the basement. While in the carriage house, TAPS members heard voices in the courtyard. A digital voice recorder left in the carriage house caught the sounds of items slamming to the ground and the voice of a woman screaming, "Get out of here. Oh, my God."

11. The Watchman of the Hamilton Inn

The Hamilton Inn of Lafayette Square was built in 1873 for prominent businessman Samuel Pugh Hamilton and his wife, Sarah V. Hamilton, and their family. As with most wealthy Savannah families, the Hamiltons were known for their extravagant parties. They were also knwn for having the first home in Savannah equipped with electricity, as Hamilton was the president of the Brush Electric Light & Power Company. The Hamilton House was a favorite of neighborhood children who enjoyed playing with the billiard table on the third floor. They would collect the billiard balls from the table and drop them, one by one, on the hardwood floors and roll them up and down the hallways.

Perhaps because of his wealth or, as some believe, shady business practices, Mr. Hamilton employed an armed guard to sit on the front stoop of his home to protect his wealth and family. One evening, Hamilton returned to his home to find that his armed guard had been shot and was lying dead on the steps of his home. Hamilton burst violently through the front door in his rush to check on his family. They were safe in their beds.

The Hamiltons eventually moved from the home, and over the years it has been owned by several different families. In the early 1990s, the home was rented by Joe Odom. He was known for his parties that raged into the wee hours of the night, having many and different guests sleeping over nightly. On occasion, he ran an electrical cord to a neighboring house, when he "forgot" to pay his utility bill.

The Hamilton House was converted into an inn in 1997. Those who have worked at the inn and many of its guests believe the spirit of the guard of the Hamilton Inn, and perhaps a few other spirits, still go about their daily lives in the home.

The watchman of the Hamilton Inn still keeps his vigil over innkeepers and guests from the inn's front stoop. Several guests have returned home late in the evening from dinner to find a man dressed in Civil War era clothing and holding a rifle sitting on the front step of the home. Staff members of the inn have experienced the front doors flying open violently when no one is present on the front steps or in the entryway.

Several guests have returned to the inn late in the evening to find a man dressed in Civil War era clothing and clutching a rifle sitting on the front step of the home. Staff members of the inn say the front doors often fly open violently, when no one is present on the front steps or in the entryway.

In addition to the watchman of the inn, guests say that the children of Hamilton Inn still enjoy their play area on the top-floor of the home. Guests who have stayed on or near the floor often hear the sounds of billiard balls hitting the floor and rolling down the hallway. They hear the happy sounds of children running and giggling in the hallways, even though the Hamilton Inn does not permit guests under the age of twelve to stay there.

12. The Doctor Is Still In

There are a handful of homes in Savannah that have been treated to the rites of exorcism by well-meaning clergy. But few were as sad as the exorcism of the doctor residing in an unassuming house on a well-traveled Savannah street. Built in 1850, the stucco-covered gray-brick home was the residence and medical office of Dr. Eugene Corsome, a pioneer in medical x-ray technology. For years, Dr. Corsome treated patients and studied the new technology from the ground floor of his home, without regard for his own health. After excessive exposure to radiation, his health began to wane. In his later years, Dr. Corsome continued to practice medicine, even as his fingers had become burned and crumpled from radiation.

In 1951, long after Corsome's death, an investor purchased the home and converted it into an apartment building. Many of the renters left after just a few months, claiming that the ghost of an elderly man without fingers was in the building. After several failed attempts to rent the home, it was turned into a storage facility and music studio. On several occasions, musicians in the studio saw the apparition of an elderly man sitting in front of a harp, moving his fingerless hands over the harp strings.

After several such encounters, the home's owner grew to appreciate the presence of Dr. Corsome's ghost. A single man with no family, the owner often ate dinner at the house. Many times, as he down for a meal at the dining table, the chair at the other end of the table would slide out and back in and the owner would say, "hello, doctor."

In 1996, the owner left the house in the care of a longtime friend and Catholic Bishop, while he traveled to another of his properties. When he returned, he found that the Bishop had exorcised his house and that his good friend, the doctor, was gone. Although he angrily demanded the exorcism be reversed, the Bishop refused. The church denied that the ceremony had taken place, but the ghost of Dr. Corsome was not seen again.

13. An Eternal Game of Hide and Seek

Isaiah Davenport and nine slaves built a fine house in 1820 on East State Street. Isaiah and his wife, Sarah, lived there until Isaiah's death from yellow fever in 1827. Sarah remained in the home for a short while after, renting rooms to provide income for herself. In the early 1900s, the Isaiah Davenport House became a boarding house with up to ten families housed in its rooms.

Now, The Isaiah Davenport House is a museum and a gift shop, but there may be a permanent resident still taking refuge within its many rooms. She made herself known to a couple of ladies visiting Savannah from New England.

Isaiah Davenport and nine slaves built The Isaiah Davenport House in 1820. It is believed to be haunted by the spirit of a little girl playing an eternal game of hide-and-seek.

The ladies had taken a tour of the home and were so entranced by the architecture and antiques that they were allowed to roam the house freely for a few moments after speaking with the tour guide and museum clerk. As they explored the upstairs, they saw a little girl in a white dress playfully running down the halls and from room to room. She seemed to be playing with them, running away just as they entered a room, and giggling at them.

When they returned to the gift shop to thank the clerk for allowing them to look around, they told her they really enjoyed the house and that they thought her daughter was adorable.

The clerk, who did not have a daughter, was concerned that someone had left a child in the house, and all three women went back upstairs to investigate.

When they reached the top floor, one of the women glanced out of the window and saw the little girl running and playing in the square just outside the house. All three women rushed down the stairs and into the square. The little girl was gone. But, as the women turned to walk back to house, they saw her again smiling at them from the window on the top floor of the house, where they had just been standing. They watched as she faded from view.

14. Aunt Clara's Last Hurrah

The Owens Thomas House that sits in Oglethorpe Square is known to be the haunt of an older woman affectionately known, both in her life and in her death, as Aunt Clara. The home was built between 1816 and 1819 for successful cotton merchant and banker Richard Richardson. George Welshman Owens, a former mayor of Savannah, also owned it.

The home's most famous resident, however, was Aunt Clara. She was known by her friends and family for her love of life and celebrations. She held lavish parties often, and especially on her birthday. Aunt Clara's birthday party was one of the most important social events of the year, and it was a tradition that partygoers wore colonial-style dress.

After her death, several of her friends and family members planned a party in her honor on her birthday and hired a photographer to capture the event. The photographer recorded attendees in traditional colonial dress with cake and punch in hand. According to Savannah legend, the photos showed an extra attendee, Aunt Clara, standing with her friends and family enjoying her own party.

The Owens Thomas House of Oglethorpe Square was built between 1816 and 1819 for successful cotton merchant and banker Richard Richardson. George Welshman Owens, a former mayor of Savannah, also owned the house. It is better known as the party home of long-past belle of the ball, Aunt Clara.

15. William Washington Gordon's Promise

Juliette Gordon Lowe is famous in and outside the city of Savannah as the founder of the Girl Scouts of America. And the house of her birth, on a corner at East Oglethorpe Avenue, is famous for another reason; it is the place of one of the most romantic ghost stories ever told.

The Juliette Gordon Low house was built between 1818 and 1821. Nelly and William Washington Gordon, a young couple very much in love, purchased the home in 1831. They had met as students at Yale University and fell in love. They were parted only when William left to fight in the Mexican American War, the Civil War, and the Spanish American War. Not wanting to part with him, Nelly joined William during the Spanish American War by serving as a nurse in Miami.

The Juliette Gordon Low house was built around 1818 to 1821. It is the site of Savannah's most romantic ghost story.

When the Spanish American War ended, the Gordons moved back to their home in Savannah. Amidst all the joy and love in the Gordon household, there was one topic that Nelly found difficult to discuss, even with William. Nelly was terrified of death. To ease her fears, William made her a promise. If he died first, he would come back for her when it was her time, take her by the hand, and lead her into the next world. In 1912, William died at the age of 78. Nelly took a great deal of comfort from his promise and often talked to their children about the day when their father would come back for her.

In 1917, Nelly had been bedridden for nearly six months and her children and grandchildren huddled around her. On the day of Nelly's death, the house was full of family. Montgomery, the Gordon's butler, was downstairs greeting well wishers. When he opened the front door, the ghost of William Gordon walked past him and up the stairs to the bedrooms.

Upstairs, granddaughter Margaret was sitting in the library reading a book when she heard someone walk up the stairs. She peeked into the hallway and watched in shock as the ghost of William walked down the hallway. He hesitated for a moment and looked at her, placing his finger to his lips as if to tell her not to speak. Then he continued down the hallway into Nelly's bedroom.

Inside the room, to the amazement of the family members huddled around her bed, Nelly sat straight up with her arms outstretched and a look of happiness on her face. Then, her eyes closed and her body fell limp on the bed. As Margaret moved down stairs to tell the others that Nelly had passed, Montgomery stood in the foyer with tears in his eyes and said, "Your daddy came home to claim your mama."

16. Advice from Beyond

Among stories of friendship and love from the other side, the story of the Espe house is a dark reminder of power, corruption, and murder. At least one of its victims sought to warn others not to fall prey to its allure.

The Espe mansion was built for Supreme Court Judge Carl Espe, a Free Mason with family ties to George Washington. He had a wife and two children, and publicly was steadfast in his belief in the prohibition of alcohol. Secretly, however, he was being paid by several gangs to cover up their black-market booze dealing. According to legend, a tunnel beneath the mansion stretched a city block hiding massive kegs of liquor.

The business of deception came to an ugly head when Judge Espe's son, William, began an affair with the paramour of a young gangster. The gang leaders warned Espe that his son was in danger, but the judge was afraid to reveal to his son the extent of his own corruption and did not pass the warning on to him. It was a decision that cost the judge the lives of both his children.

On a cold December night, William, beaten and mutilated, was deposited on the steps of the Espe house. William lapsed into a coma and died three days later. The night of William's death, his parents argued violently. Clara, the Espes' six-year-old daughter, had wandered toward them down through the home's elevator to listen. In a rage, Espe pushed over a marble-topped table. Clara's body was not discovered until early the next morning when housekeepers cleaned up the mess left from the argument.

For many years, the Espe house was used as an apartment building. Now it is owned by the Methodist Church. Through the years, William's spirit has been seen throughout the house and on the third-floor balcony. He appears in tattered clothes with a confused expression on his face.

One account comes from a family that stayed in the house. They came home to find William's spirit in the front hall. He placed his finger to his lips, as if to tell them to be quiet, and gestured for them to follow him into the parlor. He stood before them with a pained expression on his face and whispered twice, "Be just."

Civil War in Savannah

In the 1850s in the South, cotton was the most important crop and Savannah, as the port city, was full of wealth and decadence. Every responsible job was connected to the export of this "white gold" to Europe and New England.

Although the South was prospering, there were angry sentiments in the southern states over the continuation of the 1828 Mallory Bill, which many called the "Tariff of Abominations" or the "Black Tariff." The Mallory Bill raised the tariff on imported goods from Europe to fifty percent, making European imports, such as raw wool, iron, hemp, molasses, and liquors extremely expensive.

The northern states were enabled to raise their prices for the same items, and this strained the relationship between the southern states and the European cotton importers. Tensions grew by the mid-1850s as the southern states became tired of watching the profits of their labor go to the northern states. At the same time, tension surrounding the practice of slavery was brewing. While the northern states had their own cruel labor practices, including child labor and immigrants who were paid so little they often died of starvation or hypothermia on the job, the North had effectively abolished slavery and many there were judgmental toward the South.

In 1860, Abraham Lincoln was elected president of the United States. Although he was not an abolitionist by any means, he made it clear that he believed the institution of slavery should not be allowed to advance beyond its existing condition. The southern states found themselves governed by a president who did not receive a single southern vote. Before Lincoln's 1861 inauguration, South Carolina, Mississippi, Florida, Alabama, Georgia, Louisiana, and Texas seceded from the Union, declared themselves the Confederate States of America, and established a capitol in Montgomery, Alabama.

Lincoln called the secession legally void, stating that the constitution of the United States was a legal document and, as such, would require the agreements of all parties involved for any states to secede. He announced that he would use force, if necessary, to maintain possession of federal property. Lincoln rejected all negotiations with representatives of the Confederate States.[10] Union soldiers manned Fort Sumter in the harbor of Charleston, South Carolina. For a month, requests by South Carolina for the Union to evacuate the fort were ignored. In 1861, Lincoln ordered more troops and supplies to the fort and the Confederate States of America fired the first shots of the conflict, overtaking Fort Sumter. The war had begun. Lincoln called for volunteers to put down the "Southern rebellion" of secession, as Virginia, Arkansas, North Carolina, and Tennessee aligned with the South.[10]

Tensions continued to escalate with the announcement of the 1862 Emancipation Proclamation, that declared that slaves in the Confederate States of America would be freed if these states did not return to the Union by January 1, 1863. The second order, announced on January 1, 1863, named ten specific states where it would apply: Texas, Florida, Alabama, Louisiana, Arkansas, South Carolina, North Carolina, and Virginia.

Although the Proclamation did not immediately free any slaves because the states it listed were all under the control of the Confederate States of America, it put the issue of slavery on the fore front, and politically established the North as anti-slavery and the South as pro-slavery, a public-relations strategy that ensured that France and England, which had abolished slavery years earlier, would not be coming to the aide of the southern states. Union soldiers used the Proclamation to free slaves in the territories they conquered and to topple the southern economy. [11] By 1864, General William Tecumseh Sherman was methodically making his way through the South, burning cities to the ground; destroying residents' homes, churches, and businesses; and along with them, their history and culture. He began his trek through Georgia announcing, "I can make the march and make Georgia howl." [11]

17. A City Saved – for Love or Money?

One of the best known facts about Savannah is the destruction the city avoided during the Civil War. Sherman had destroyed Atlanta by burning buildings, dismantling railroads, and cutting telegraph wires. As he continued marching east toward the shore, people around Savannah braced themselves for the worst. But, when the General arrived, he seemed in spirits too good to destroy the city, instead offering it to President Lincoln stating, "I beg to present to you, as a Christmas gift, the city of Savannah, with 150 heavy guns and plenty of ammunition, and also about 25,000 bales of cotton."

Sherman was prepared to do damage to Savannah, arriving with 65,000 troops to Savannah's 10,000, according to records. What interrupted him from his rampage?

Many believe Savannah was saved because of the southern hospitality of a very beautiful young belle. After hearing about the destruction in Atlanta, she greeted the general kindly and offered him "womanly comforts" if he would spare her city. The general agreed, and after a night of passion he left her, her home, possessions, and city intact, then went on to devastate Charleston.

Another story suggests that Sherman never intended to destroy Savannah because it was home to a woman he once courted and loved very much, but who had married another man. In yet another story, a Mother Superior beseeched him to spare her city. As a God fearing man, he could not ignore her request. Others believe the general entered the city with every intention of destroying it, but once there he was so taken by its beauty that he could not bring himself to destroy it. He took what weapons and horses he could use and moved north to Charleston. Locals say this is the least likely reason of all, because Sherman was known as an egotistical maniac whose opinion was rarely swayed by anything without concrete value.

Most people now believe the city was spared because of its sheer number of houses of ill repute. Once Union soldiers arrived in the city, the General could not burn any buildings because he had no idea in which of them his soldiers were engaged.

The truth may be a combination of all these reasons. General Sherman was greeted by the Mayor of Savannah and a delegation that offered to surrender the city without a fight if it was not burned. Sherman accepted the offer.

This was a strange fate for a city that was steeped in a war-time culture that believed that any southerner who cooperated with Sherman was disloyal and considered a collaborator with the "Northern devil."

Many cities in Sherman's path had surrendered, yet suffered the same consequences as those that had not.

Sherman stayed in Savannah for a short time commandeering ammunition and horses. He left Savannah untouched and continued his rampage north, burning the city of Charleston to the ground.

Historians today suggest the most likely reason Savannah was saved had more to do with politics than with passion or politeness. They believe Savannah survived for a handful of reasons. When Sherman arrived in Savannah, there was cotton in the harbor; he would not have risked losing the cash crop. His troops were coming to the end of a long winter campaign and they had been held up in Fort McAlister, in Richmond Hills, for several days without fresh supplies. Christmas was coming and it would be easier to take a break and freshen the troops in an intact city. But more importantly, it was an election year and Lincoln wanted the country to be supportive of the war. The press reported Sherman's destructive march through the South and there was anti-war sentiment growing in the North. Sherman could not risk reports that he destroyed a city that so easily surrendered.

As Sherman's 65,000 soldiers flooded the city, generals commandeered many of Savannah's finer homes while enlisted men took shelter where they could find it. They set up camps in the city squares, parks, and the Old Colonial Park Cemetery. In their effort to set up tents for themselves and provide space for items they had stolen along the way and for their horses, they knocked down many tombstones. It was a bitter, rainy winter and soldiers broke into crypts to stay warm. They dumped bodies from the shelves so they could sleep curled up on dry crypt shelves. In their boredom, they looted graves, re-arranged gravestones, and scratched into gravestones with their bayonets; so that many bodies in the cemetery are recorded as having died before they were born or having more than a hundred children.

18. What the Yankees Missed

Savannah families hid their belongings during the Civil War anywhere they could—in carved-out compartments of walls, bed mattresses, even sewn inside ladies' skirts. In one legend, a gentlemen hid all his belongings inside a dried well on his property. He covered the well to keep it from the approaching troops, and fled the city; but when he returned he found his house untouched. He realized in his haste to leave he had not documented the location of the well, and spent many nights digging in his yard for his belongings.

In fact, Union soldiers were so feared in Savannah that families not only hid their valuables, but their daughters as well. The Mackey family lived on the outskirts of Savannah. When news came that General Sherman and his soldiers were approaching, they feared for the safety of their beautiful young daughter. They hid her in a secret compartment within a wall, with her pet chicken and several of the family's valuables, and covered the wall with boards. They were concealed together with the understanding that if the chicken began to make noise, she would have to silence it any way she could. Sherman's troops arrived at the house and took what they could of the family's belongings. As they were leaving, they heard strange sounds coming from inside of the wall. They began pulling the boards from the wall, but just as they were about to reach the girl and the family's valuables, they were called away.

Many Savannah women refused to be frightened by the men invading their homes. It is said today that while the capture of the city was taking place, Sherman remarked of Savannah women, "If the Civil War was fought by women, it would never end."

During his stay in Savannah, General William Tecumseh Sherman settled into the Green-Meldrim House of Madison Square for a less than restful stay.

Historical records and diaries of the time indicate that the women of Savannah were proud, strong, and in no mood to give up their silver, their jewels, or their city. If they could not stop the soldiers, they were at least going to show them what Savannah women were made of. Sherman, himself, grappled with the unwavering combative attitude of several of Savannah's women during his stay.

Sherman settled into the Green-Meldrim House of Madison Square, beside St. John's Episcopal Church. The owner of the home, Charles Green, thought it better to welcome the enemy into his home than have it destroyed. It worked out well for Green, but others were outraged.

When the ladies of St. John's Episcopal Church found out that Sherman was staying so close to their place of worship, they decided that he would not be getting any rest. They set up a 24-hour vigil at the church and prayed, sang hymns, and rang the church bells every fifteen minutes, morning, noon and night. They hoped to expedite the departure of the man they referred to as "the living devil."

In response, Sherman ordered his soldiers to remove the bells from the church, with plans to have them melted down and used to create ammunition, as he had done with other church

Above: According to legend, General William Tecumseh Sherman was confronted by an angry Southern lady on the porch of the Green-Meldrim House, who told him that he and his soldiers were "thieving louses" and that he could expect a daily visit from her until her family's possessions were returned.

Opposite: Members of the congregation of the St. John's Episcopal Church, next to the Green-Meldrim House, set up a 24-hour vigil at the church. They prayed, they sang hymns, and they rang the church bells every fifteen minutes—morning, noon and night—in the hope of expediting the departure of the man they referred to as "the living devil."

bells throughout the South. What Sherman didn't know was that one of the offending ladies was a member of the wealthy Faye family that had donated the bells to the church, and that she was a close friend of Mary Todd Lincoln. Faye wrote a letter to Mrs. Lincoln explaining that soldiers had taken away their church bells. Shortly after, Sherman was ordered by President Lincoln to place the bells back in the church. Sherman did as he was ordered, but he held onto the bell clackers.

Once at the Green-Meldrim House, Sherman was visited by a very angry young lady who claimed that his soldiers had ransacked her home and stolen her jewelry. The servant who opened the door would not let her enter to make her complaint to the general in person. But the angry young lady refused to leave. She waited outside of the house until, eventually, Sherman stepped outside. She cornered him on the porch, telling him what louses his soldiers were to steal a lady's family jewelry. She told him that he could expect a visit from her every single day until her jewels were returned. Sherman decided it was not worth the hassle. He wrote a description of the missing items and found the soldier who had taken them. All of her jewelry was returned.

Sherman's troops ran into another young lady during their raids that would not stand for the ransacking of her home either. The young woman was alone in the home when the soldiers arrived and began rummaging through the family's belongings. The daughter of a Free Mason, she knew many of the secret hand signals. She signaled to the soldiers hoping that one of them would be a Free Mason and stop the ransacking out of honor. One of the soldiers in the group was in fact a Free Mason. He requested the other soldiers to leave this house untouched. They agreed begrudgingly, and the family's belongings were saved.

Other families were spared home invasion because of their unique connections to powerful Union generals. The

Gordon family had ties to the North that proved especially valuable. Although William Gordon was a Confederate officer, Nelly Gordon, the matriarch of the family, was born to the Kinzies, a very powerful Northern family with ties to Sherman. Nelly and Sherman had never met, they had exchanged letters as children. Because of that connection, during the occupation of Savannah, Sherman paid a social visit to the Gordon home and brought with him another general, Oliver Howard, who had suffered a battle injury that resulted in the loss of one of his arms. The men were welcomed into the Gordon home and shown into the parlor where they were greeted by Nelly and the Gordon's four-year-old daughter, Juliette. The child bounded into the room playfully and jumped into the lap of General Howard, at which point she noticed his missing appendage. She looked up at him curiously and said, "what happened to your arm?" Howard replied gruffly, "I was wounded in battle and they had to remove it." Juliette looked at him and matter-of-factly replied, "I shouldn't wonder if my papa did it! He has shot a lot of Yankees."

The prevailing notion at the time was that Union troops would not damage property of Union supporters or Confederates who welcomed them to stay in their homes as guests. This belief did not work out well for British Consul Edmund Molyneux. He believed his status as a non-Confederate would secure the protection of his home and the vast wine, art, and furniture collections within it. Unfortunately for Molyneux, General Howard and his men discovered the house and its contents. They drank every drop of his wine and destroyed much of his property. Molyneux filed an $11,000 lawsuit against the United States for the damages, but his efforts were ignored.[12]

19. Nora Foley's Yankee

As the Civil War came to a close, Southern women found themselves widowed and trying to support themselves and their households; many opened their homes as boarding houses. If that didn't bring in enough money, some offered additional services to gentlemen guests. Nora Foley was left more comfortable than most of the Southern women widowed by the war. Her husband had left her with a small fortune with which Nora purchased a boarding house on Chippewa Square. According to legend, one evening a Yankee who was staying at the home decided he was in need of some "additional" services, and he was going to get them whether or not Nora was offering. He crept up to her room in the late hours of the evening and approached her in her bed. Nora heard him coming and was ready to whack him with a lamp from her bedside table. The two struggled and Nora hit him so hard in the head that he died on her bedroom floor.

Another guest, a man by the name of Richard, a brick layer who had been staying in the home because his house on Tybee Island had recently been destroyed, heard the struggle and rushed to Nora's aid. That night, a Yankee was encased inside a brick wall of the Foley House. Nora and Richard were married a few short weeks later. The story of Nora Foley's Yankee was just Savannah folklore until nearly 100 years later.

In 2001, the owners of the Foley House purchased the building next door and began to renovate it. As they worked to knock down a wall between the two homes, they noticed that the 18-inch thick brick wall was not load-bearing. As they knocked through it, out dropped the mummified remains of a Union soldier.

Nora Foley, of the Foley House of Chippewa Square, is known for having killed a Union soldier in self-defense and encasing his body in a hollowed wall of the Foley House.

Love of Libations,
The Wettest City
in the South

In 1733, when the settlement of Savannah was established, the city was "dry" of rum per its creator, Edward James Oglethorpe. Oglethorpe felt liquor would demoralize the colonists. The decree did not sit well with colonists. They argued with Oglethorpe that the humid weather and hard toil of living in the newly established colony required the comfort of rum. They sneaked it in from the booming neighboring settlement of Charleston. Eventually, when they could not convince Oglethorpe to change his mind about their beloved booze, they accused him of mistreating and mismanaging the colony and developed a public relations campaign that included a widely circulated pamphlet about Oglethorpe's mismanagement. The pamphlet made its way to England, where Oglethorpe was tried and cleared of mishandling. At last, the colonists legalized their beloved libation.

20. Evergreen Bonaventure Cemetery – The Eternal Party

To this day, Savannah is well known for its lavish parties and hospitality among the living and the dead. People love to explain with a devilish half-smile that what counts in Savannah is not from where your family hails, or where or if you go to church, but what you would like to drink.

The story that best represents Savannah's spirit of hospitality and residents' love of celebration takes place in the city's Evergreen Bonaventure Cemetery. In 1762, the Mullyrne

A row of trees at the entrance to the Evergreen Bonaventure Cemetery may be those planted by John Mullryne. As legend has it, Mullryne had the trees lining the plantation entrance sculpted to form the letters M and T, to celebrate the wedding of his daughter Mary Mullryne to Josiah Tattnall. Many believe today that enough of the original trees remains that, if you concentrate, you can still see the outline of the letters.

family, Colonel John and Claudia Mullryne, established their home on 600-acres about three and a half miles from the colony of Savannah. The couple named their home Bonaventure, French for "good fortune." The mansion burned down in 1771, and the family built an imposing brick mansion in its place. The Mullrynes' youngest daughter Mary later married Josiah Tattnall, and they came to Bonaventure to live in the family estate. As legend has it, Colonel John was so happy with the match that he had trees planted along the drive that intertwined to spell M and T, to symbolize the melding of the two families as one. Many believe that enough of the original trees remain that if you concentrate, you can still see the outline of the letters.[13]

According to historical records, the mansion was destroyed by fire between 1803 and 1817. According to legend, the fire took place during a lavish party the family was hosting on the grounds. Fire consumed much of the mansion's attic and roof. A butler nonchalantly leaned over and whispered to the host

Evergreen Bonaventure Cemetery is the final resting place for the Tattnall family, famous for continuing to entertain guests in the garden of the Mullryne-Tattnall plantation as their grand home burned to the ground.

that the home was on fire. He calmly rose from his seat, lifted his glass, and invited his guests to join him for drinks in the garden. The servants carried the tables and food out to the garden where the guests finished their dinner and drinks by the light of the burning mansion. Many visitors to Bonaventure say if you listen closely, you can still hear the laughter and tinkling glasses of that eternal party.[14]

By 1846 the property was owned by Commodore Josiah Tattnall III. He sold the 600 acres, excluding the Tattnall family burial ground, to prominent businessman Peter Wiltberger for five thousand dollars. Seventy acres at the northeastern corner of the land were designated as the Evergreen Bonaventure Cemetery. Since then, hundreds of well-known Savannah residents have been interned on its peaceful grounds.

21. Prohibition –
Rum Runners and Gas Station Taverns

For locals, prohibition didn't seem to register with any importance. The fact that liquor was illegal simply changed where they got their libations, and for some, even added an air of mischievousness to the ambiance of social gatherings that have always been a staple of Savannah society. Among the many oft-visited Savannah speakeasies was the Pirates' House, on East Broad Street. Rum runners easily could slip the illegal drink into the tunnel system that runs beneath the building and store it in any of the seemingly ubiquitous secret walls and compartments of the house and basement.

Other known speakeasies include a gas station on Abercorn Street, where drivers could fill their gas containers with whiskey; an unassuming restaurant on West Jones Street, that is now known as the Crystal Beer Parlor; and a marina called Green's.

Patrons of Green's would stage a party on the front grounds of the marina with music and dancing. The noise and their bodies blocked from view the rowboats stocking the back room with liquor.

The area along Wilmington Island was a drop-off destination for rum runners. They would deliver cases of liquor by rowboat late in the evening and hide them in the marsh where they were later picked up and delivered to speakeasies across the South. Rum runners also dropped off their supplies at homes on Whitmore Shallaw, Richardson Creek, and Willington Creek Island, where gangsters would row out and meet them at sea to take the supplies to the shore.

One of the most popular speakeasies in Savannah, Bo Peep's, once stood at 17 Congress Street. The building has since been torn down and paved over to serve as a parking lot for Christ Church. Bo Peep's belonged to a man named Wolfe. He was the son of English and German immigrants who arrived in Savannah in 1902. Wolfe was 21 when Prohibition was enacted and he saw a need to continue to supply his community with what he referred to as the "water of life."

Wolfe traveled to New Orleans where he met and partnered with a gangster, Bugs Moran, who imported the needed "water" into New Orleans. Wolfe started bringing pint bottles in suitcases, then barrels by the carload. When he needed a point of distribution, he rented space on Congress Street, and Bo Peep's was born.

The restaurant and speakeasy was known for its relaxed atmosphere, its pool tables, and the best roast-beef sandwiches in town. Wolf's business was booming. He bought a dozen Cadillacs for their size and weight and before taking them on the road to New Orleans, he drove them in circles on a dirt track to camouflage them with dirt. On one of his trips to New Orleans, several of the Cadillacs were pulled over by police. Wolfe sped home to the speakeasy without them. A

Among the many often-visited Savannah speakeasies, the Pirates' House on East Broad Street, was where rum runners easily could slip their illegal drink into a tunnel system that runs beneath the building.

patron commented, "Little Bo Peep has lost his sheep," and the speakeasy was known as Bo Peep's from then on.[15]

It is said that Bo Peep's was so successful and well-known that local police officers and officials would occasionally stop by to take a bribe. More than once a preacher from the nearby Christ Church stopped by, collection plate in hand, and remarked, "Let me hold some of that money. The devil has had it long enough."[15]

Those were the heydays in Savannah of Al Capone and his henchmen. Capone was born in Brooklyn, New York, on January 17, 1899. He quit school at the age of fourteen and joined the notorious Five Points gang of Manhattan. He worked in gangster Frankie Yale's Brooklyn bar, The Harvard Inn, as a

There the liquor could be stored in any of the seemingly ubiquitous secret walls and compartments of the house and basement.

bouncer and bartender. There he received his famous facial scars in a barroom brawl and earned his nickname, Scarface.[16]

Capone soon went to work for Yale's mentor, John Torrio. By 1922, Capone was Torrio's right-hand man managing his bootlegging business, saloons, gambling houses, and brothels. By 1925, Capone controlled speakeasies, bookie joints, gambling houses, brothels, horse and race tracks, nightclubs, distilleries, and breweries.[16]

In the late 1920s, Capone expanded his business into Savannah. Capone and gang members drove around the city in pickup trucks customized for crime with hidden compartments for cases of liquor and padded shocks to hide its weight. Capone called his customized fleet of vehicles "Shoe Salesmen." Much of that customization was done by Savannah mechanic and owner of the Helmey garage, Sherman I. "Moose" Helmey.

In 1928, Moose was a law-abiding man running a small automobile repair shop on State Street in his hometown, Savannah. He was a businessman and a ladies' man, known for his charm and charisma, innovative mechanical skills, and genteel sense of discretion – characteristics that made him the perfect partner in crime.

On a warm spring evening in 1928, Moose got an invitation to put his skills to work. A black Ford truck stacked with fresh vegetables pulled slowly into the parking lot of Helmey Garage. Two men stepped out wearing denim work overalls, outfits that seemed to Moose to be in contrast with their determined expression and purposeful gait.

The driver of the truck was a short, balding man with a round face and an intense gaze. He stared at Moose for a moment, as if he was sizing him up, then he said, "You work on Fords?" It wasn't a question. Moose inspected the truck while the men went into the garage office. They returned moments later wearing crisp black Tuxedos with tails and shiny black leather shoes.

"What the truck needs is a new transmission," Moose explained. "But a new truck like this should be under warranty. There is a Ford dealership just up the stretch. They'll be able to fix you up. You don't want us to work on it. You could get a new truck for what it would cost us to fix it."

"I don't care about that," the man answered. "Can you fix it?" Then Moose realized he was talking to Al Capone. And that "Can you fix it?" wasn't a question either.

"When it's done," Capone said, "deliver it to the Desoto Hotel and leave the keys at the front desk."

Moose's mechanic took the truck into the garage. After several hours, Moose went to check on the progress. He found his mechanic drunk and passed out on the garage floor beside an opened crate full of bottles of liquor. It was one of many crates of liquor stacked beneath mounds of vegetables.

Moose thought, "They are going to kill me." He pushed the mechanic aside, completed the work on the transmission, and placed what was left of the liquor back into the crate beneath the vegetables.

In the morning, Moose drove the truck to the Desoto Hotel. He handed the key to the clerk at the front desk and turned to leave. "You Mr. Helmey,?" the clerk asked. "Yes, "Moose replied. "The gentleman would like to see you in his room."

Moments later Moose was standing in a hotel room with Al Capone. "You know who I am?" Capone said.

"Yes, I do," said Moose.

"Would you like to do some more repairs for me?" asked Capone.

"Yes, I would," said Moose.

From that day on, Helmey Garage was the busiest repair shop in Savannah, and Moose was officially a gangster.

He greeted his customers in custom suits and blue suede shoes. His mechanics worked continuously repairing a parade of Cadillacs and Lincoln Continentals with bullet-riddled radiators and cracked windows from "hunting accidents."

Moose customized their cars with hidden compartments for stashing cases of liquor. He added felt pieces to the springs and strips of shoe leather to the stocks to keep them from looking as if they were carrying a heavy load.

Moose also had a special relationship with several of Savannah's finest. He paid any police officer a cash bonus that brought him a wrecked vehicle.

Not everyone in Savannah was comfortable depending on speakeasies for their supply of liquor. According to legend, several groups, including some of Savannah most elite ladies, paid their own crew of rum runners to supply them with a continuous shipment from Cuba.

A Pirate's Life for We

During the 1700s, piracy at sea was a way of life for many. For those who enjoyed it, there was more than enough to pillage and the city of Savannah was a great place to stop for grog and to shanghai a crew member or two.

22. The Pirates' House, Inspiration for Treasure Island

The Pirates' House was built in 1753, a block or so from the Savannah River, as an inn and tavern that welcomed seafarers to the city. The house was well known as a place to find comfort after months at sea, for both travelers with legitimate business in the area and for pirates.

Locals say The Pirates' House, on East Broad Street, was specifically mentioned in Robert Louis Stevenson's classic novel Treasure Island. To them, *Treasure Island* is more than a classic work of fiction, it is a story inspired by real-life events, many of which took place in Savannah at the Pirates' House, with real-life pirates who considered Savannah their stomping ground. Stevenson's *Treasure Island* is set in the mid-1700s, when pirates like Black Bart, Calico Jack

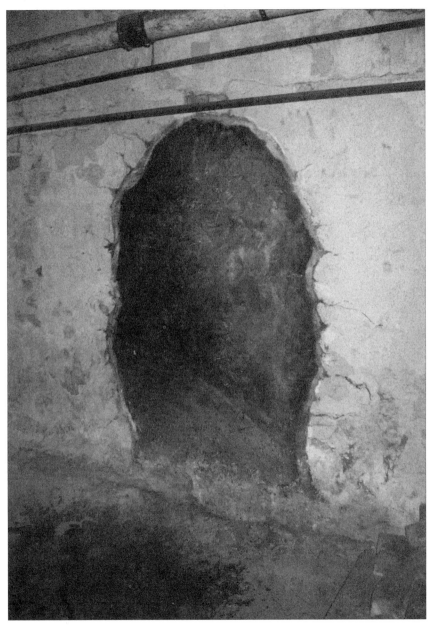

Pirates wanting to kidnap tavern patrons used the underground tunnels of the Pirates' House.

Patrons who were drunk or otherwise incapacitated often were thrown into the basement and dragged through the long tunnel system to a waiting ship.

Rackham, Samuel Bellamy, Anne Bonney, and Mary Read sailed the seven seas and stopped into Savannah for a quick libation and a crew member or two.

23. The Tunnel to China

As with many of Savannah's parties, the good times at the Pirates' House were not always a good time for all. In addition to offering seafarers a warm room, food, and ale, the Pirates' House offered adventure many were not in the market for. The Pirates' House was built with several secret compartments and a stone tunnel leading from the dining room to the basement. According to history and local legend, innkeepers used such compartments and passageways to abduct guests and sell them into a life of forced piracy for $12 a piece. Area pirates new the Pirates' House was a good place to replace crew members that had died at sea or in battle. Innkeepers waited until a patron passed out from drink and shoved them into a wall compartment or the underground passageway. Additionally, innkeepers might lure-in the poor with the promise of food or liquor and knock them over the head and throw their body into the tunnel. Pirates who were not interested in waiting for warm bodies, went into the streets and picked up one or more of the myriad orphaned children begging in the street and offered them a life of adventure and treasure. Those who awoke unexpectedly at sea were given choices: work as a pirate, or die today by walking the plank with cannonballs tied to your feet, or take a final swim in shark-infested waters.

24. Pleading the Belly

According to historical documents dating from the mid-1700s, it is likely that several historically significant pirates visited Savannah during this time, including the infamous lady cross-dressing pirates Anne Bonney and Mary Read, who, legend says, were not above revealing their breasts in the midst of battle to distract their enemies.

Mary Read was born in England. Her mother was married to a sailor from a wealthy family who apparently was not ready for fatherhood. He set sail and never returned. Mrs. Read gave birth to a baby boy. But, shortly after his birth, and with a husband clearly out of town, she found herself pregnant again. She packed up her family and relocated to a village in the country where her son died, and she gave birth to a baby girl she named Mary. She did not tell anyone about the death of her son or the birth of her daughter. [17] From birth, she taught Mary to pretend that she was a boy. When she was four years old, her mother took her to London to visit her husband's mother and request financial assistance. Her mother-in-law welcomed mother and daughter warmly, completely convinced that Mary was her grandson. She requested that the two move to London and live with her. Afraid that Mary would be discovered under those living arrangements, Mrs. Read convinced her mother-in-law that she needed to return to her job in the village, but that a crown a week would be sufficient financial support.

As a teenager, Mary learned to bind her chest with tight clothes to hide her breasts and was careful to wear clothing that did not reveal her feminine body. Eventually, her grandmother died and the money stopped. But Mary continued to live as a boy, even joining the Royal Navy. [18] Later, she joined the crew of a Dutch merchant vessel. The ship was captured by an English pirate by the name of Charles Vane who gave Read – as the only other "Englishmen" on board – the option of joining his crew as a pirate. Read accepted the offer and joined Vane as a pirate. According to legend, their ship was captured by the infamous "Calico" Jack Rackham and Anne Bonney, another female pirate passing herself off as a man. Bonney was well-known as a cruel and murderous pirate. Bonney and Read developed a strong attraction and revealed their true identity to each other.

According to accounts, Bonney and Read were close friends, perhaps even lovers. That is what Rackham believed. He and Bonney had been close for months before Read's ship was captured, and his suspicion was mounting that Bonney was in love with the Read "boy." When Rackham angrily confronted the two about their behavior, Read smiled at him and barred her breasts. [18] Another legend claims that Read fell in love with a young navigator the crew had captured and the two became lovers. When he and another crew member argued and decided to settle their dispute the gentlemanly way, a duel was planned. Mary then challenged her lover's adversary to a duel and the two met off the ship early in the morning. Read killed him and returned to the ship and her love.

The robberies and murders came to an end when Read's and Bonney's ship was attacked in Jamaica by British naval captain Jonathan Barnett. Read and Bonney were such fierce fighters that they took on the invaders, while the other pirates, including Rackham, hid below deck. Read shouted down the hull for them to come and fight. When they did not, she fired her guns into the hull and killed and wounded her own crew members. [19]

It took more than an hour for the British to subdue Bonney and Read. The crew was taken to Port Royal, Jamaica, where a short trial found them guilty of "piracy, felonies, and robberies... on the high sea." Rackham and his men were hanged. Read and Bonney were given the same sentence, but informed the court that they were both "with child," and according to British law could not be executed. The defense is known as "pleading the belly." They were jailed until they could be hanged. Mary grew ill and died, while Bonney escaped and was never found. [20]

Anne Bonney, Mary Read, and their motley crew were not the only pirates sailing the Savannah coast. The infamous pirate Blackbeard also frequented Savannah on his ship, *Queen Anne's Revenge*. Blackbeard is described as a towering man with a stern face buried beneath mounds of thick, black unruly facial fair. He wore a crimson-colored coat stuffed with weapons, including two swords at his waist and bandoliers across his chest packed with pistols and knives.

He preyed on lightly armed merchant ships in shallow water off of the coast of North and South Carolina and Georgia.

Blackbeard intimidated his foes by sticking cannon fuses beneath his hat and lighting them during brawls.[21] He stowed his plunder on Sapelo Island, also known as "Blackbeard Island," 16,500-acres just 60 miles from Savannah. [17]

Despite Blackbeard's reputation and intimidating appearance, according to historical documents he was not a cruel man. Most of his victims did not put up a fight. He took their rum, valuables, and weapons and let them sail away. If they resisted, however, he burned their ship and left the surviving crew marooned. No historical evidence claims that Blackbeard killed anyone who was not trying to kill him. [21] Blackbeard met his death at the hands of the Royal Navy on Ocracoke Inlet, North Carolina. Lieutenent Robert Maynard collected a bounty of six hundred pounds of silver for lobbing off Blackbeard's head. Legend has it that the head of Blackbeard traveled on the ballast of Maynard's ship to authorities in Virginia and was placed on a stake near the mouth of the Hampton River as a warning to other pirates.

Camouflaged by Culture

In the mid-1700s, war was brewing in the northern colonies of America. The southern colonies remained mostly ignored by British troops until 1778, when British forces turned their attention to Savannah. They saw Georgia as an important part of the American colonies since it was home to many loyalists of England and was not heavily defended. British Lieutenant Colonel Archibald Campbell was ordered to invade Georgia with 3,000 troops to restore the colony to British rule and set an example to other southern colonies.[22]

Although rumors circulated that slaves might be freed after the war, they continued to be viewed as property. Throughout the British occupation of Savannah, soldiers and colonists used slaves as currency. They were taken in raids and offered to soldiers as payment for services. Considered to be spoils of war, slaves were often taken to plantations far from where they were born to live and work for years. Some were killed in battles and many took advantage of the confusion to disappear and make a new life elsewhere. It has been estimated that 15,000 slaves ran away successfully during the American revolution.[22] Few runaway slaves were captured because they found ingenious ways to be elusive. Runaways took advantage of the common fear of disease by telling their captors they had been hiding with escapees who had Small Pox. This claim almost always resulted in captors getting as far away from the slaves as possible.

Plantation life returned nearly to normal after 1782, and rumors that slaves would be freed after the Revolution were unfounded. They realized they would have to find their own way to freedom. Some believed it would come through the grace of God, others from the ground beneath their feet. For many, it was both.

25. Truthiness Shall Set You Free

Of all of the stories of people who have outsmarted their adversaries and lived to tell about it, those of slaves in the American South are some of the most heroic. As the turmoil of the Revolutionary War ended, many slaves turned to evangelical Christianity to find stability and strength in new ways to communicate. Many slave owners encouraged slaves to adopt a Christian lifestyle and ideals. Some had a genuine concern for their souls while others felt the basic principles of serving your master, turning the other cheek, and receiving your rewards in the next life worked well to keep slaves content in their bondage. Churches encouraged slaves to attend services, stressing the belief that slavery was part of the natural order of things.[23] The Bible gave support to these ideas:

> Slaves, obey your earthly masters with fear and trembling, in singleness of heart, as you obey Christ; not only while being watched, and in order to please them, but as slaves of Christ, doing the will of God from the heart. (Eph. 6:5-6)

Tell slaves to be submissive to their masters and to give satisfaction in every respect; they are not to talk back, not to pilfer, but to show complete and perfect fidelity, so that in everything they may be an ornament to the doctrine of God our Savior. (Titus 2:9-10)

Slaves, accept the authority of your masters with all deference, not only those who are kind and gentle but also those who are harsh. For it is a credit to you if, being aware of God, you endure pain while suffering unjustly. If you endure when you are beaten for doing wrong, what credit is that? But if you endure when you do right and suffer for it, you have God's approval. (1Pet. 2:18-29)

Who then is the faithful and wise slave, whom his master has put in charge of his household, to give the other slaves their allowance of food at the proper time? Blessed is that slave whom his master will find at work when he arrives. (Matt. 24:45-46)

Occasionally, slaves heard sermons that preached ideas clearly counter to their owners' beliefs, such as "you had better go home and set your slaves free," to which many slaves laughed and sneered. The hypocrisy of the owners and contradictions in the church helped slaves believe they were more Christian and closer to God than their masters. For those who had recently arrived in America or been taught by those who remembered their lives in Africa, the Christian idea of the Father, Son, and Holy Spirit was not very different than tribal gods. [28]

Christian slaves in Savannah gathered at night for prayer meetings without hypocrisy. Preachers emerged with language and dialog that only the slaves could understand, which enabled them to hold "secret" meetings in the open with whites in attendance. These meetings became an impetus for change. Black ministers found they could travel with white preachers and preach different messages depending on who was listening. Although black preachers could speak English well, they chose to speak in dialect that slaves understood and whites viewed as ignorant. [28] Sermons such as ""De Sun Do Move An' De Earth Am Square" were successful at communicating different messages to different people. Heretics preached that the earth rotated around a stationary sun. The sermon stated, "Joshua tell de sun ter stand' still till he could finish whippin de enemy an de sun was travellin' long dar thew de sky when it stops for Joshua. It stopt fer business an' it went on when it got thew." [28] While whites in the audience giggled at the ignorance of the preacher, slaves understood he was telling them that God can intervene in the natural order of things. Ignorant whites would be damned for keeping people in bondage. When black preachers told the story of Adam and Eve, Adam was frightened by his sin and turned white. [28] Besides communicating hope to each other through religious sermons, slaves communicated for a better future and specific information how to escape through their songs. For instance, "We'll soon be free when da Lord call us home," and "O Canaan, sweet Canaan, I'm bound for the land of Canaan" meant the North. [28]

In Savannah and northern Georgia, runaway slaves looked for symbols. A painted black coachman figure holding a lighted lantern meant they had reached a safe house. If the lantern was dark, they knew to keep moving. Runaway slaves also looked for symbols on bed quilts hanging from windows and porch balconies encoded with messages. The Jacob's Ladder pattern, a combination of four-patch and half-square triangles, was hung outside homes of underground railroad supporters. In this climate, a handful of slaves decided to build a church that would offer religious expression to many and freedom to the brave.

26. There Is Freedom Beneath the Floorboards

A slave named George Leile established The First African Baptist Church in 1777. It was known at the time as the first "colored" Baptist Church in Georgia. The church served as a sanctuary for those seeking spiritual support and guidance, and it served as an escape route for slaves seeking a new life.

Carvings on the pews of the First African Baptist Church are believed to be symbols from tribal languages carved into the pews by slaves who built the church. *Photograph by Arminpa Hairston of the First African Baptist Church.*

A slave named George Leile established The First African Baptist Church in Savannah in 1777. It was known then as the first "colored" Baptist Church in Georgia and Leile was the first black man licensed to preach in the Baptist religion in Georgia. He was a popular preacher among slaves living on plantations along the Savannah River.

Leile settled in Savannah and built a congregation of slaves and free black people. In 1822, the congregation built a sanctuary on Franklin Square. Slaves worked during the day for their masters and then on the church at night. The women carried Savannah gray bricks a half-mile from Hermitage Plantation where slaves made the bricks by hand. They kept a bonfire burning as the men carved wood and built the pews. They decorated the pews with symbols of their homeland tribes. A large tree trunk runs through the roof of the chapel, from end to end, supporting lighting fixtures.[29]

A patchwork pattern in the chapel ceiling mimics the symbolism of the Jacob's Ladder pattern for the Underground Railroad. The walls of the sanctuary were painted haint blue and the floorboards were decorated with diamond-shaped, African tribal, prayer symbols. These symbols were important tools to help church members connect to their heritage and lifelines for runaway slaves who hid beneath the floorboards of the sanctuary. There, beneath the prayer symbols, were shallow spaces with just enough room for a person to lie down; the holes of the prayer symbols provided fresh air. Food and water could be slipped through the holes discreetly during prayer ceremonies. Many escaping slaves traveling up the Savannah River stopped for a night at the church. They hid under the floorboards until abolitionist guides arrived to help them. The guides arrived for a ceremony with four black companions and walked out of the front door when it was over with five.

The floorboards of the First African Baptist Church are decorated with African tribal, diamond-shaped prayer symbols. The symbols were important tools to help church members connect to their heritage, their hopes, and their faith. They were also lifelines for the runaway slaves who hid beneath the floorboards of the sanctuary. *Photograph by Arminpa Hairston of the First African Baptist Church.*

Love, Sex and Murder in the Days of Slavery

T hey say that the first Africans brought to Savannah to work as slaves were the strongest of the men. And of them, those who survived the journey from Africa to the Georgia shore were the bravest and the healthiest. Documents from the time describe them as having great physical strength, broad shoulders, strong rippling muscles and skin as smooth and clear as the night and as dark as fireplace pitch.

As the story goes, many of the ladies living on the plantations of Savannah found these young strong men working bare-chested in the sun and just steps from their bedrooms, more than a bit distracting. The plantation owners soon decided it would be a good idea to bring some female slaves to the colony to offer companionship to the male workers. In most cases, plantation women behaved themselves and the male slaves avoided temptation. But for some, the draw of the forbidden was just too great.

27. The Curse of Francis Sorrell

Francis Sorrell was born in 1793 in Saint Dominique, Haiti, the son of Antoine Sorrell, a white sugar cane plantation owner and retired French Army Colonel and a free black woman. In the 1791 Haitian slave uprising, Antoine fled to Cuba, leaving Francis and his mother to fend for themselves. After his mother was killed, Francis was raised by his mother's family.

In 1812 Francis became an apprentice to a businessman and the two traveled to Savannah to become cotton agents.

The Sorrel Weed House was the home of the cursed Francis Sorrel, his wife Matilda, and his lover Molly.

Molly, a slave at the Sorrel Weed House and Francis Sorrel's lover, was the only slave at the Sorrel House with private living quarters above the carriage house.

Here he became immersed in the business, building wealth and a name for himself. Francis disowned his African family and denied his mother and bloodline, a decision that, according to local legend, started a voodoo curse that followed him for the rest of his life and killed every woman he ever loved.

By 1823, Francis had become disconnected from his Haitian and African roots. He had cut all family ties, built a profitable empire as a wealthy cotton trader and property owner, and taken a fancy to young Miss Lucinda Moxley.

The two wed and had three children. After several years of marriage, Lucinda became mysteriously ill and died suddenly at the age of 29. Francis kept his family intact by marrying Lucinda's sister, Matilda, and for years they enjoyed a happy life, producing eight more children. Francis moved his family into the Sorrell Weed House in 1838, a 16,000 square foot showplace on newly established Madison Square. The family was well known for lavish parties that began in the home's front parlor and spilled into the open space of the square in late evening hours.

The Sorrell family had more than thirty slaves, some of whom lived in a carriage house behind the mansion. Others were commissioned to work at local plantations. The Sorrels treated their slaves well and considered them extensions of the family, but a slave named Molly was held in higher regard than the rest. She was Matilda's right-hand woman in running the Sorrel household, her confidant, and closest friend. Molly was the only slave at the Sorrel Weed House with private living quarters above the carriage house. She was especially skilled at planning formal get-togethers. It was her job to prepare for the lavish Sorrel-family parties. In fact, there were things that Molly attended to in the Sorrel household of which Matilda was unaware, until one early Spring afternoon.

After finding her husband, Francis Sorrel, in the arms of their slave Molly, Matilda Sorrel walked across the courtyard, into the mansion, and launched herself off her bedroom balcony onto the courtyard outside of Molly's window.

The household was abuzz with party preparation. Servants scrambled about moving furniture, preparing food, and adjusting decorations. Matilda noticed that Molly was not directing the servants as she usually did, so she searched the house and walked across the courtyard to the carriage house and up to Molly's room. Matilda cautiously tapped on Molly's door and waited, then cracked the door and peaked inside. Molly and Francis were making love in Molly's bed. Matilda quietly closed the door, walked back across the courtyard, into the mansion, and launched herself off of her bedroom balcony to her death.

Francis mourned the death of his wife for three weeks. He locked himself in his bedroom and refused visitors. But after his solitude, he could not resist visiting Molly. He crept out to the carriage house in the dark of the night and slid open her door. He found Molly hanging by a noose from the rafters. Although there was no stool or chair beneath her feet, Molly's death was ruled a suicide. Francis suspected his sons in her murder. Stricken with grief, he sold the family house and purchased and moved into the house next-door. Although he lived just feet away from the courtyard and carriage house where he had lost the three loves of his life, Francis lived on in a home with no windows and no balconies.

28. Mary Telfair's Keeper

In the early 1800s, Mary Telfair was the young daughter of distinguished Savannah residents Edward Telfair, the Governor of Georgia, and Sarah Gibbons, a member of one of the wealthiest and most prominent families in the South. Mary had endless choices, except as with all women of the time, she was expected to marry.

A proponent for the arts, Mary was known for her love of travel and helping people. She spent her life traveling and volunteering for causes. But as the years passed, she never took a suitor and showed no interest in marrying. It was the desire for the freedom to devote her life to her causes that she said kept her from marrying. But those who knew her and her travel companion, a slave named George Gibbons, knew that it was her relationship with George that kept her from entertaining male suitors. Mary is remembered as the benefactor for establishing the Hodgson Hall building that houses the Georgia Historical Society, founding the Mary Telfair Hospital for Women, and establishing the Telfair Academy of Arts and Sciences. George had strong ties to the Underground Railroad through his membership and eventually pastor position with the First African Baptist Church. With his connections, George could have easily escaped to freedom. George and Mary spent their lives together traveling and helping those less fortunate. The two were never separated until her death at the age of 84. In her will, Mary left George seven thousand dollars.

29. The Murder of Mr. Wise

Young and pretty Alice Riley arrived in Savannah in December of 1733, along with her husband Richard, to serve as indentured servants to William Wise. Wise was known for making "unorthodox" requests of his servants, including his daily baths and grooming sessions that required the participation of several female servants and, always, Alice Riley.[30]

On a warmer than usual March morning, Alice decided that she had had enough of Mr. Wise. She waited until it was time for his bathing. As he lay in his bed relaxed with his eyes closed, Richard emerged from his hiding place and the two of them grabbed Mr. Wise and held his head into his bathing bucket until he drowned. They fled the house together to the Isle of Hope, just off the coast of Savannah. [30]

Days later they were found and sentenced to death by hanging in Justice Square. Richard was hanged immediately. Alice continually maintained her innocence and was found to be pregnant, so the courts waited eight months for her to have her baby and then hanged her in the square. Her body was left hanging on display for three days. [30]

Legend maintains that the odd absence of Spanish Moss on the trees of Wright Square is due to the unjust hanging of Alice Riley. And, accordingly, that Spanish Moss does not grow where innocent blood has been shed. [30]

Business As Usual

From the early history of Savannah, the business of keeping up appearances has permeated the culture of the wealthy and not-so-wealthy alike. For some, it is maintaining a façade of wealth by adding painted faux-marble baseboards and crown molding to the front rooms of the home. For others, it is living on "the street" where only the wealthy can afford to live. Still for others, it is protecting their pride with compromise and shotguns. Negotiations are always about who has the most to risk and who has the least to lose. In Savannah, the business of wealth, idealism, and appearance can be a dangerous game between the haves and the have-nots. Those who are willing to risk it all, often lose it.

30. The Dueling Grounds – Compromise in the Colony

In the early days in Savannah there were many things to quarrel about—politics, religious freedom, and whether one had or had not gotten a glimpse of a lady's ankle whilst she walked up the stairs, in which case, of course, he could be ordered to marry her. Any of these topics were considered reasonable disagreements

An epithet in the Old Colonial Park Cemetery marks the final resting place of one of many who died fighting for their own cause on the dueling grounds of Savannah.

to end with, "Sir, I challenge you to a duel." The proper thing to do once a challenge was made, was to meet at the Dueling Grounds for a fight to the death. Although dueling was not legal in Savannah, the accepted belief was that, "a man may shoot the man who invades his character, as he may shoot him who attempts to break into his house." [31]

Many idealistic Savannah gentlemen lost their lives defending their pride, including a signer of the Declaration of Independence, Button Gwinnett. Gwinnett lost a duel to Lachlan McIntosh on Savannah's Dueling Grounds. The two had a history of antagonism toward one another.

Between 1700 and 1808, when two men could not come to agreement nor could they agree to disagree, they met at the city's dueling grounds to shoot it out until only one man remained standing. The small tract of land beside the Old Colonial Cemetery served as the city's dueling grounds.

One of many tombstones of a man who fought and died on the dueling grounds of Savannah. The grave sits in Savannah's Old Colonial Park Cemetery.

The double staircases of the Isaiah Davenport House, built in 1820, are examples of social customs inspiring architecture. In the 1800s, if a gentleman happened to catch a glimpse of a lady's ankle while she was walking or climbing a set of stairs, her father or brother could argue that the gentleman should either marry her or face a duel. For this reason, many homes were built with dual staircases, one side for ladies and one for gentlemen.

Gwinnett arrived in Georgia from England in the early 1760s. He ran a failed general store in Savannah and then tried his hand at farming nearby St. Catherine's, a coastal island. [32] When that too failed, he turned to politics. In 1767, he served as a Georgia Justice of the Peace and later he served in the state's Lower Assembly. By 1774, Gwinnett had become outspoken about England's "Intolerable Acts" toward the colonies. His radicalism annoyed the conservative and wealthy merchant Lachlan McIntosh, and the two soon became enemies. In 1776, Gwinnett was elected by the Assembly as a Georgia delegate to the assembly in Philadelphia where the Declaration of Independence was drafted. [32] Gwinnett returned to Georgia where he ran for election to be commander of the state's militia, but he lost the position to McIntosh. He was, however, elected to be Georgia's Speaker of the House and played a fundamental role in writing the Georgia Constitution. McIntosh criticized the document, stating that it gave, "power...to irresponsible and avaricious individuals and groups." [32]

When Georgia Governor Archibald Bulloch died, Gwinnett was elevated to the position of Governor by the Assembly's Executive Council. In 1777, he ran for re-election to the position, but lost to John Adam Treutlen.

When McIntosh openly criticized him, Gwinnett challenged McIntosh to a duel. The men fought in the small town of Thunderbolt, near Savannah, and Gwinnett received a shot to the leg that shattered his bones. He died three days later of gangrene and was laid to rest in the Old Colonial Cemetery. [32] McIntosh went on to enjoy a successful political career until his death in 1806. He too is buried in Old Colonial Park cemetery, just a few feet from Button Gwinnett.

31. The Mercer House of Monterey Square – Death and Antiques

Well-told stories of business, pleasure, and death revolve around the Mercer House of Monterey Square, one of the grandest, most beautifully restored, and infamous homes in all of Savannah.

The massive brick home sits proudly on the corner of Bull and East Gordon Streets on Monterey Square. Its strong stone steps reach out to the square to welcome passersby, as if the deaths that took place within its walls and on its steps have been forgotten and the gentile parties that once raged long into evening hours still fill the night air with laughter and the clinking of fine glassware.

Before it was the site of a grisly murder and the untimely death of one of Savannah's most beloved antique dealers, Mercer House was just another antique home in need of repair and set for demolition. Armstrong College planned to level the home to build a gymnasium.

The Mercer House of Monterey Square was the home of Arthur James "Jim" Williams, a man famous for the restoration of many Savannah homes and infamous for his implication in the death of Danny Hansford and for his own mysterious death.

In the late twentieth century, James Arthur "Jim" Williams was an experienced restorer of antique homes, having saved more than fifty throughout Savannah. Like many other talented men, Williams' death shed light on the way he lived his life. Williams died on January 14, 1990, from a heart attack. The Mercer House was Williams' last project.

Legally there was no murder committed in the Mercer House or on its grounds. But as the story goes, Williams lived in the home alone and ran a successful antiques shop in the home's carriage house. Williams was also known for throwing lavish parties for Savannah's elite and wealthy, and other more intimate parties for a select group of Savannah's finest gentlemen. Among those who knew him well, Williams was known for dabbling in voodoo and his close friends believed him to be a gifted psychic.

Legend has it that Williams had been tested by a group of researchers at Duke University and found to have exceptional powers of Extrasensory Perception (ESP). He often engaged visitors at his home with a game he called "psycho dice," where each player attempted to increase the odds of winning by concentrating on controlling the outcome of a roll of the dice. He was also a close friend and frequent client of voodoo priestess, Valerie Fennel Aiken Boles.

Williams employed the services of a young man, Danny Hansford, who helped him in his antique restoration business and with whom he may have had a romantic relationship. The day Hansford was found dead in the living room of the Mercer House, Williams' fingerprints were found on the antique German Louger gun that had killed him. Williams' only defense was that Hansford was prone to fits of rage and on that particular evening Williams felt his life was being threatened. Williams related that on the evening in question, Hansford was raging out of control, smashing furniture and screaming profanities. Hansford grabbed an antique gun and fired at Williams. Williams did not deny killing Danny, but claimed it was an act of self-defense. Williams was charged with murder and housed at the Chatham County jail. Throughout his trial ,several oddities about the night Hansford died came to light. According to phone records, Williams called a friend before he called 911 in the moments after Hansford was shot. And, photos of the crime scene showed a table leg resting on a section of Hansford's pants, suggesting that the crime scene was staged.

Nevertheless, Williams was acquitted of the murder, returned home to Mercer House and turned his attention to his antiques business. According to witnesses, Williams and Ms.

Boles later had a very public argument, and six months later Williams walked out of his front door and felt the pangs of a heart attack. He collapsed on the front steps of Mercer House and died. The official cause of William's death was the heart attack, but those who knew of his relationship with Ms. Boles say he was most likely "dusted by the blue root." According to legend, there is a blue root in South Carolina that voodoo practitioners use to cause sudden death. It is so poisonous that touching a bit of root dust with one finger is enough to cause instant death, and it is completely untraceable post-mortem.

If a voodoo practitioner has been hired to kill you with the root, they may visit your home while you are away and sprinkle the root on your toilet seat or the remote control to your television. When you touch those things, the root dust will cause a massive and sudden heart attack. Other practitioners prefer a more public death, hiring children to carry a needle filled with the dust. The child rubs the needle on your hand or arm and you die almost immediately.

Jim Williams has become part of the folklore surrounding the Mercer House. Some people in Savannah believe that Hansford was murdered in the home, but that it wasn't necessarily Williams who did the killing. People who have lived in Savannah a long time have known of the Mercer House before Williams' restoration of the property and believe that the Mercer House has an evil all its own. They say Mercer House has been home to many murderers.

For example, the father of Johnny Mercer, who is synonymous with popular music, such as the songs "Goody Goody," "That Old Black Magic," and "One for my Baby" (and "One for The Road"), was the home's first owner. His great-grandfather, Hugh Mercer, was known for something less pleasant. Hugh Mercer was the patriarch of the Savannah Mercer family in the mid-1800s. He served as a Confederate General in the Civil War where he was charged and imprisoned for the murders of two army

In 1902, the second owner of the Mercer House – whom many suspected of having murdered his wife – walked out onto the Mercer House balcony, tripped, and fell over the railing. He plummeted more than 50 feet to the sidewalk below, instantly breaking his neck.

deserters. He was eventually acquitted, mainly on the testimony of his son. According to legend, he returned to Savannah in 1868 an angry and bitter man and sold Mercer House to John Wilder, who completed the house to its 10,000-square-foot specifications.

In 1902 an elderly couple purchased Mercer House. One evening, the man reached over in his sleep and attacked his

In 1969 Tommy Downs broke into the Mercer House and climbed out of a window onto the roof. He climbed to the highest peak and pulled out a slingshot to aim at one of the pigeons resting on its eaves. Downs lost his footing and fell 70 feet onto the metal fence that surrounds the house, breaking off one of the decorative metal fence tips.

wife, smothering her to death with a pillow. He was tried and acquitted of the murder. Two weeks later, the man walked out onto the Mercer House balcony, tripped and fell over the railing. He plummeted more than 50 feet to the sidewalk below instantly breaking his neck. Mercer House was bequeathed to the Shriners. It served as their temple for 39 years. The House seemed to be at peace until 1969.

By the late 1960s, brothels and men's fraternity houses had surrounded the Mercer House, which had fallen into decay. It was a favorite playground for area children who snuck in through broken windows to explore its ruins. In 1969, the Mercer House took another victim. On a Sunday afternoon, Tommy Downs broke into the Mercer House and climbed out of a window onto the roof. He climbed to the highest peak and pulled out a slingshot to aim at pigeons resting on its eaves. He lost his footing and fell 70 feet onto the metal fence that surrounds the house, breaking off one of the decorative metal fence tips.

In 1970, Jim Williams purchased Mercer House and restored it. The home is now the private residence of Williams' sister, Dorothy. The first floor of Mercer House is open to the public during the day. Visitors can walk through the study where Danny Hansford was shot and killed, stand in front of the door that Jim Williams opened before he clutched his chest and tumbled down the front steps, touch the still-broken fence tip that took Tommy's life, and view a portrait of the acquitted Hugh Mercer that hangs nonchalantly on a sitting-room wall.

The Girls Are Alright

Among the characters of Savannah, some of the bravest, most talented, and most eccentric have been ladies. They challenged the status quo and became quirky permanent fixtures of Savannah's folklore and legend.

32. Tomo Chi Chi Rocks On

Wright Square is the final resting spot of Tomo Chi Chi, the leader of the Native American village of Yamacraw and trusted friend of Savannah founder, General James Edward Oglethorpe. Originally a pile of stones in the Yamacraw tradition marked Tomo Chi Chi's grave. In 1899, it became evident that the stones needed to be replaced with a monument.

When wealthy resident Nelly Gordon heard that Tomo Chi Chi's stones were going to be replaced by a non-stone statue, she volunteered to donate the money to pay for a large stone monument. She contacted The Stone Mountain Monument Company who offered to supply the stone for no charge. Ms. Gordon felt that she was being condescended to and insisted on paying. The Monument Company sent her a bill for 50 cents payable on Judgment Day. Ms. Gordon paid the bill and sent with it a note that read "On Judgment Day I will be occupied with my own affairs."

33. The Birth of the Girl Scouts of America

Ms. Nelly Gordon's daughter—Juliette Gordon Low or "Daisy" as her favorite uncle named her—was born on Halloween night in 1860 to Nelly and William Gordon. Juliette was known for her creativity, artistic talent, and a stubborn streak that could not be conquered or accept

The Juliette Gordon Low House was the home of Juliette Gordon for her childhood and much of her adult life.

compromise. Juliette showed exceptional artistic talent at an early age. She often repainted portraits of family members, including transforming a portrait of her father into her great-grandfather. She also sculpted a bust of her father and painted it bronze. She was known for carving designs into furniture around her home that she felt was too plain.

At the age of 26, Juliette married Willy Low, a multi-millionaire who owned a successful shipping business in

Juliette and Willy Low were married at Christ Church in Savannah. It was while leaving the ceremony at this church that Juliette was struck in the ear with a grain of rice contributing to her lifelong deafness.

England. The two married at Christ Church on Johnson Square and held their reception at her childhood home, now called the Juliette Gordon Low House. As the couple was leaving the church after their wedding, Juliette was struck in the ear with a grain of rice. The doctor who removed the grain punctured her eardrum and she lost hearing in that ear. Later, she lost hearing in her other ear from an infection and was left 80-percent deaf. After founding the Girl Scouts of America years later, she would often say that she never heard anyone say "no" when she asked for money for her scouts.

The couple moved into the Andrew Low House of Lafayette Square for ten months as they made plans to move to England. It was traditional at the time that the family's gardens were hidden behind brick walls, because it was considered improper to see a lady sweat and toil in the sun. Juliette laid out her garden in front of the house so all could see how hard women worked to sustain their homes.

As Juliette prepared to leave Savannah and join her husband at his home in England, she knew that she would miss her mother, so she asked to take the painting of her that was hanging in her parents' front parlor. When her father refused to part with it, Juliette purchased a canvas and recreated the painting. In England, Juliette noticed the beautiful iron gates that decorated many of the manor homes. Rather than purchase gates for her home, she visited a local blacksmith and learned how to manipulate raw iron. She then designed and built a set of gates for her new home.

After several years of marriage, Juliette learned that Willy had a mistress. Juliette refused to divorce him, but she returned to her childhood home in Savannah and began searching for something to bring purpose to her life. During one of her trips through England, she met the founder of the Boy Scouts organization. He mentioned to her that he had

Juliette and Willy Low lived in the Andrew Lowe House of Lafayette Square for ten months as they made plans to move to England. Despite the tradition of the time that ladies did not work hard or sweat, Juliette laid out her garden in front of the house, so all could see how hard women worked to sustain their homes.

received 6,000 applications to join the Scouts that he could not accept because they were from girls. Juliette contacted the girls and the Girl Guides of England was born. Juliette returned to Savannah and partnered with her cousin, who ran a girls school, to create the Girl Scouts of America.

Juliette Low designed the Girl Scout uniform similarly to the Boy Scout uniform, and used the colors from her home for the Brownie and Girl Scout uniforms. Juliette wore her Girl Scout uniform almost every day.

While living in England with her new husband, Juliette noticed the beautiful iron gates that decorate many English manors. Rather than purchase gates for her own home, she visited a local blacksmith and learned how to manipulate raw iron. She then designed and built a set of gates for her home.

After five years of marriage, her husband, Willy, died and left his estate to his mistress. Juliette took on the British courts and won a sizeable settlement.

When Juliette died in 1927, there were 168,000 Girl Scouts in America. Today, troops from around the country pilgrimage to the Juliette Gordon Low House every year to pay homage to Juliette Gordon Low.

34. Framing Mrs. Wayne's Rear

In 1820, long before the Gordons had moved into their home on the corner of Oglethorpe and Whitaker streets, that would someday be known as the Juliette Gordon Low house, the home was owned by Judge James Wayne and his wife. The Waynes were completing renovations on the home, including building an addition to the rear. Mrs. Wayne had a reputation for being difficult to please, and after several redesigns she was still displeased with the addition.

Mrs. Wayne, the architect, and the builder all stood together looking at the rear of the house in a complete breakdown of communication. The very proper Mrs. Wayne looked at the men and said, "I can't imagine what it is you do not understand. I want two three story levels on each side," to which the architect replied, "And how would you like that framed?" Very irritated, Mrs. Wayne sighed loudly, turned to her side and replied, "Oh, just build it like my ass."[33]

35. The Waving Girl of River Street

Between 1887 and 1931, Florence Martus lived with her brother, George, who served as the lighthouse keeper at the entrance to the Savannah Harbor. Florence and her little dog spent the days waving in ships as they entered the port. At night, the little dog woke her when a ship was approaching.

According to legend, Florence had fallen deeply in love with a merchant sailor who promised to someday return to Savannah and marry her. She stood by the river and waved her handkerchief to welcome every incoming ship and waved goodbye to every out going ship. She became such a fixture that seamen referred to Savannah as "the girl's house." They would whistle and salute her as they pulled into port. After Florence Martus died, the Savannah Altrusa Club raised funds to have a statue built in her honor so that she could forever wave the ships into Savannah's port. The statue was constructed by sculptor Felix de Weldon (the same sculptor who created the bronze image of Marines raising the flag at Iwo Jima that stands proudly at the entrance to the Marine Corps headquarters in Quantico, Virginia).

Although there is no indication that Florence Martus was more than friendly with any of the seamen who frequented the port of Savannah, some snicker that the sculpture is the only statue in the world erected to celebrate someone's mistress.[34]

36. Prostitution and Propriety

The services of prostitutes have always been available in Savannah. There are boarding houses whose innkeepers or staff offer a little something extra to their well-paying guests; and escort services known only to elite members of society who have solid resources and a sophisticated sense of discretion. There are streetwalkers and ladies of the evening who sit patiently in bars waiting for propositions. And there are sophisticated networks of call girls known only to bellman and concierge staff of luxury hotels. Locals say that a network of highly paid prostitutes still operates at Ardsley Park, one of Savannah's most prestigious neighborhoods.[35]

But throughout the years, there have been a handful of places where a gentleman was assured of a good time. Indian Lil's was situated on Indian Street, two blocks south of the Savannah River, where the United States Post Office

A statue of Florence Martus, the "Waving Girl of River Street," still greats ships from River Street. Between 1887 and 1931, Florence Martus lived with her brother, George, who served as the lighthouse keeper at the entrance to the Savannah Harbor. Florence and their little dog spent their days waving in ships as they came into port. At night, the little dog woke her when a ship was approaching.

According to legend, Florence had fallen deeply in love with a merchant sailor who promised to someday return to Savannah and marry her.

now stands. Lillian Sims and her brother, Joe, ran Indian Lil's. They also ran a couple of other houses of ill-repute on West Broad Street, across from the Fire Station.35 Several brothels have been on Congress Street.

According to local legend, Ma's Place – actually a string of oft-visited brothels owned and operated by Mamie Saxe – was the best place in town to gain a little companionship on a lonely evening. There were Ma's Places located on the southwest corner of Montgomery Street, West Broad Street, Oglethorpe Avenue, and Liberty Street.[35]

Savannah native Tom Coffey was a newspaper delivery boy when Savannah's brothels were in full swing. Legend has it that madams and prostitutes were known to be the best tippers, because they always had lots of cash at hand. If you were so inclined, they were also willing to pay "with the trade."[35]

Savannah's houses of ill repute were fitted with false walls hidden inside closets so that, in the case of a raid, customers could be stowed away. Police officers who raided the homes were often unsuccessful, and left standing outside scratching their heads as to how there were so many cars parked outside the brothel and not a single man inside.[36]

As raids became more frequent and the brothels began to shut down, Ma's Place by the railroad caught fire, possibly by the hands of an uppity arson. The house was badly burned in the fire and subsequently closed. The only evidence of its past proclivity was a note tacked to the front door that read, "Closed. Beat it."[35]

Revenge in the City of the Dead

As much as Savannah is a city that celebrates the lighter side of the human spirit, a place of eccentric people, lavish parties, and wealth, it is not immune to the darker of the human emotions, especially jealously, rage, and revenge.

37. Poison in the Water Supply

In the late 1980s, the citizens of Savannah were terrified by a shy and slightly unstable man who claimed to possess a vile of poison so potent that if he dropped just a bit into the water supply of Savannah it would kill every man, woman and child. According to local legend, the ingenious inventor of the flea collar and the no-pest strip was an irritable man who felt powerless in his life and expressed his frustration by conducting morose experiments on insects and by letting it be known to all that he possessed the power to poison everyone in the city. [36]

He had been a technician with a government position in Savannah, where he tested insecticides by injecting them into the chest cavities of various insects. In his free time, he was known to entertain himself by gluing threads to house flies, sometimes walking down the streets of Savannah holding onto the threads of a half-dozen or so flies. He had also been known to glue the wings of a wasp to the wings of a fly to improve its aerodynamics.

During his employment with the government, he had made the discovery that a certain pesticide could pass through plastic, which had many profitable applications. Because he was a government employee at the time, he had no claim to the discovery. His only options were to turn the discovery over to his employer or sell it secretly to a private manufacturer. While he was thinking it over, one of his colleagues learned of the discovery and beat him to action. According to local legend, the mysterious and mad scientist still roams the streets of Savannah holding onto the strings of insects and looking for a little bit of respect.[36]

38. The Beast-man of Old Colonial Park

For as long as there have been parents and children, parents have taken advantage of the lore of the boogeyman, warning children that if they don't behave, some mythical creature will "get them." A boogeyman exists in many cultures. In England there are bog men who rise from the moors as zombies. In Brazil it is the *hombre de la bolsa* or *del saco* who comes to collect the children who should be home in their beds, and in Germany *Der Swartz Mann* hides in dark places—in closets and under beds—awaiting the chance to grab naughty children and whisk them away.

The boogeyman of Savannah is known as René, or "the Beast-man of Old Colonial Park Cemetery." The Beast-man is a large, looming, and shadowy figure that skulks around the city at night looking for victims. But it always returns to its home in the Old Colonial Park Cemetery, which is where it prefers to exact its crimes against the city's inhabitants.

René was not always the Beast-man. In the early 1800s, René was just a young and awkward boy living in colonial Savannah. As legend has it, he spent his days playing in the Old Colonial Park Cemetery befriending the cemetery groundskeepers, who were leery of him, as was everyone else. They became suspicious of René after discovering mutilated bodies of animals in the cemetery. Although they suspected him of the crimes, they looked the other way until they stumbled upon the body of a mutilated young girl.

The boogeyman of Savannah is known as René, or "the Beast-man of Old Colonial Park Cemetery." The Beast-man is a large, looming, and shadowy figure that skulks around the city at night looking for victims. But it always returns to its home in the Old Colonial Park Cemetery, which is where it prefers to exact its crimes against the city's inhabitants.

Savannah's Marriott by the River sits at the approximate location of where René, the Beast-man of Savannah, was hanged by an angry mob in the early 1800s.

The groundskeepers and other men from town went on a manhunt for René. When they found him, they tied him to the back of a horse and buggy and dragged him through the streets of Savannah, eventually hanging him at the current site of the Marriott by the River. The men and townspeople were happy with the "justice" that had been exacted, and were relieved to have the awkward René out of their city. Several weeks later, Old Colonial Park Cemetery groundskeepers found the mutilated bodies of two more girls. In more than 200 years since René's murder, townspeople have reported seeing a seven-foot tall shadow man roaming the cemetery at night. Throughout the years, there have been many bodies found in the Old Colonial Park Cemetery and many people have vanished within its bricked walls, never to be seen again. According to legend, a tall, awkward boy named René still spends his evenings seeking revenge on the city that rejected him.

39. Dr. Buzzard and the Voodoo Priestess of Savannah

Savannah is a bastion for spirits of the dead and the undercurrent of energy in which they exist. If there is anyone who knows how to navigate the underworld for herself and the bidding of many clients, it is Valerie Fennel Aiken Boles. According to local legend, Ms. Boles is a direct descendant of Marie Laveau, the voodoo queen of New Orleans and daughter of voodoo priestess Old Mocha, who lived for more than 125 years. Boles practiced a type of voodoo called Geeche, that derived from a practice in Africa in the 16th and 17th centuries. Geeche is a combination of African voodoo and Christian practices. The Geechee voodoo priests (or root doctors) are known as Dr. Buzzard, a name that legend relates came from the first root doctor to arrive in the Americas, a man as powerful and as patient as a buzzard.[37]

Ms. Boles, who became a root doctor when her husband (the area's Dr. Buzzard) passed away, has been providing voodoo services in Savannah for more than thirty years. She lives in a small, unassuming home just over the state border in South Carolina. Those who know her say she is not an easy woman to access; only her clients know her exact location. Locals say meeting her comes at the end of a long and winding journey and involves meeting her many "helpers," who are students of voodoo. Her clients are not permitted to touch or even pay her, but put their money on the floor or table for her to retrieve at a later date.

Among the services Ms. Boles has offered over the years include protection and revenge. She can sentence your rival lover to be "ridden by the Hag," or to die suddenly, through the use of black candles and incantations. Those in need of this service light Ms. Boles' black candles and for three days, with little food or water, concentrate their energy on the death of their rival. When the candles burn out, the victim is dead.

40. The Riding of the Hag

Even in a city that embraces lust and values pleasures of self-indulgence, there are lines that are not to be crossed. When they are, consequences include penance, often in the darkest hours of the night.

In Savannah, the sin of tempting a woman's love interest comes with the most wicked atonement. For a rival who is schooled in the voodoo traditions that permeate Savannah, the Hag may greet you. According to voodoo tradition, the Hag is an evil old lady turned inside out; meaning she can change from one thing into another. For example, she can become a bird and fly through your bedroom window. She can take the form of a snake and slither into your home through an open door. The Hag will wait quietly in your home until you are sound asleep, then pounce on your back and "ride you" until you became unconscious from exhaustion or die.[38]

The legend in Savannah is that "the Hag" is sent by voodoo practitioners to settle disputes of the heart. Those who feel they have been wronged can call upon the Hag to seek their revenge. Hags are all around us, hidden behind the skin of family members, co-workers, acquaintances, and close friends. A Hag is someone you trust explicitly. They are demons that have fallen to earth from battle. They have been given human form and the capacity for happiness, but to they do not contain happiness, they must suck it from their prey.

When you lay in bed at night, the Hag is drinking your happiness. When called to action to exact revenge, a Hag rises from its body leaving its skin behind. It attacks a victim's body, climbs on top of them, and holds them down so they cannot breath, move, or scream. This is the Hag "riding you."

There have been many reported incidences of the Hag attacking young women in Savannah. In the 1990s a young art student lived in an apartment near her classroom buildings and worked at night as a bartender in the historic district. She developed an affinity for a young man who frequented the bar, and on several occasions aggressively sought his attention, even though she knew he was involved with another woman.

One night she lay in bed in her apartment listening to heavy rain pound the roof and walls and lightning crack and boom nearby. Then she heard boxes topple over and footsteps in her room. Before she could move, she felt hands on her and was pulled to the edge of the bed and flipped onto her stomach. A heavy pressure pressed into her back with such force that she could not speak or scream for help. Eventually, she was able to gather enough breath to squeak out "God, help me." When she did, the weight was lifted and she was able to run for safety.

Silly Savannah Facts

41. Skinny Escape

A man who was serving a long sentence in the county Jail lost enough weight to slide through one of the very skinny windows and escape to freedom.

42. Run-down Sundial

Tipsy or distracted drivers have plowed the sundial at the center of Johnson Square down four times. It has been struck twice since 2005.

43. A Visit from Mr. Washington

George Washington visited the city of Savannah in May of 1791. He stayed at the site of the First Chatham Bank.

The Sundial of Johnson square has the following caption: "The sundial at the center of Johnson Square has been run over and plowed down by tipsy or distracted drives four times. It has been struck twice since 2005."

44. Keeping Up with the Joneses

Jones Street of Savannah is one of two streets in the city that still has the original brick that was laid by Irish immigrants in the 1850s. Savannah residents wanted the street to be paved quickly, so the city offered a challenge to bricklayers: the man who laid the most brick in one day would win a gold coin. More than twenty bricklayers laid bricks for the street in just a few hours.

Jones Street at one time was considered one of the wealthiest streets in Savannah. It was a great show of wealth to own a home on Jones Street. Those who could not afford to live there coined the phrase, "Keeping up with the Joneses."

45. Savannah Gray Brick

Savannah gray brick was made by hand by slaves from the Hermitage Plantation, just outside Savannah. In the 1800s, gray brick was considered the poor man's brick and red brick made in factories in England was considered the rich man's brick.

Many homes in Savannah have bases of gray brick that have been stuccoed-over to hide the "inferior" brick. Today, Savannah gray brick is worth as much as $50 to $200 per brick. Many of the bricks are marked with the fingerprints of the men who molded them.

Gray Brick is no longer made; some say because the recipe was forever lost, while others claim that only one slave knew how to make the bricks and he died without passing on the knowledge. Still others say the gray clay that was used for the bricks has been fully mined.

Tomo Chi Chi, chief of the Yamacraw Indians, was rumored to stand more than seven feet tall, have only one good eye, and wear a cape of bear skin. Tomo Chi Chi is buried in Wright Square, with a large boulder marking his resting place.

46. Life Is Like A Box Of Chocolates

Actor Tom Hanks played Forest Gump in the movie *Forest Gump* and sat on a bench in Chippewa Square for the famous "box of chocolates" scene. A replica of the bench can be viewed at The Savannah History Museum.

47. Mercer House Movies

Several movies have been filmed at the Mercer House of Monterey Square, including *Midnight in the Garden of Good and*

Evil, *Swamp Thing*, *Swamp Thing*, *Return of the Swamp Thing*, and *Glory*. If you view *Glory* with a watchful eye, you can see a palm tree outside of the window, a strange occurrence for a film set in Boston.

48. The Savannah Theatre of Chippewa Square

The Savannah Theatre, built in 1818, is the oldest continuously running theatre in the United States. Junias Brutis Booth and his son, presidential assassin John Wilkes Booth, were famous actors at the Theatre.

The Savannah Theatre, built in 1818, is the oldest continuously running theatre in the United States. Junias Brutis Booth and his son, presidential assassin John Wilkes Booth, were famous actors in the theatre.

49. Bull Street

Bull Street was named for William Bull, a surveyor from Charleston, South Carolina. Locals claim they have a line of Bull that runs through the city and ends up right at City Hall.

50. Inspiration for Walt Disney World's Haunted Mansion

Cartoonist Walt Disney visited Savannah in the 1950s. He was so taken with the design of the Hamilton Inn that he walked around it and took sketches of the house. From those sketches he framed the idea for the design for the Haunted Mansion ride at Disney Land and Walt Disney World.

Cartoonist Walt Disney visited Savannah in the 1950s and was so taken with the design of the Hamilton Inn that he walked around and took sketches of the house. From them, he got the idea for the designs of the Haunted Mansion ride at the Disney Land and Walt Disney World amusement parks.

51. Pineapple Surprise

The pineapple is a southern symbol of hospitality. In Savannah, a pineapple would be placed in a prominent location in a house, such as on a fireplace mantel. If a guest awakened to find that the pineapple was gone, he was to take notice that his welcome was wearing thin.

52. Sleep Tight In Eternal Rest

Historians say the brick tombs of the Old Colonial Park Cemetery were built to resemble beds with head and footboards, to ensure their inhabitants an eternity of restful sleep.

Historians say the brick tombs of the Old Colonial Cemetery were built to resemble beds, with headboards and footboards.

Henry Ford's first showroom in the South was located at Bull Street in Savannah. The building was originally a barn for Arabian horses. Ford enjoyed the symbolism of the location, as he believed his cars would put the horse and buggy out of business.

53. Henry Ford's Savannah Showroom

Henry Ford's first showroom in the South was located on Bull Street in Savannah. The building was originally a barn for Arabian horses. Ford enjoyed the symbolism of the location, as he believed his cars would put the horse and buggy out of business.

54. Bradley's Store

Bradley's Store of State Street has been owned and operated by the Bradley family since it opened in 1883. The store's

Bradley's store of State Street has been owned and operated by the Bradley family since it opened in 1883.

The store craftsmen made a false tooth with a hidden key for Harry Houdini.
"We sharpen anything but your wits and we fix anything but a broken heart."

fame was assured when it once supplied a false tooth with a
hidden key for magician Harry Houdini. The store motto is,
"We sharpen anything but your wits and we fix anything but
a broken heart."

55. Jingle Bell Church

James L. Pierpont, the music director for Savannah's
Unitarian Church of Oglethorpe Square, wrote the classic
American Christmas carol, "Jingle Bells."

56. The Presidents Quarters Inn

The Presidents Quarters Inn has extended an invitation
to every president of the United States since the building was
converting into an inn in 1987. So far, no president has ever
stayed there.

James L. Pierpont, the music director for Savannah's Unitarian Church of Oglethorpe Square, wrote the classic American Christmas carol, "Jingle Bells."

57. Baptists Don't Burn – They Just Get Fired-up on Sunday

The Independent Presbyterian Church of Ellis Square was burned down in two major fires and knocked down by a hurricane. The Baptist Church, just next door, has never burned down.

Quite a scandal at the time, the Presbyterians suspected the Baptists of burning down the church to add to the Baptist congregation, but the Baptists claimed it had more to do with their church being built with limestone.

58. Boys Will Be Girls– Eli's Cotton Gin

Eli Whitney developed the cotton gin at the Mulberry plantation of Savannah. According to legend, Whitney was excited about his invention and wanted to show it to someone, but feared that his idea would be stolen. He decided to only share the unpatented invention with women, who he felt would not be capable of reproducing it.

Whitney unwittingly revealed his invention to a mechanically savvy man who had come to the plantation dressed as a woman in hopes of seeing the invention. The man returned home and reproduced the gin.

References

1. "Religion and the Founding of the Republic," www.loc.gov/exhibits/religion/rel01.html, Published by the Library of Congress.

2. "Biography of Tomo Chi Chi," www.tomochi-chi.org/History/history.htm, published by Savannah Online Now.

3. Elizabeth Carpenter Piechoccinski, *The Old Burying Ground, Colonial Park Cemetery, Savannah, Georgia 1750-1853*. Published by The Oglethorpe Press Inc., Savannah, Georgia, 1999, pages 1-5.

4. "Online Virtual Tour of Savannah–Wright Square," www.ourcoast.com/tours/savannah/wright.shtml , Published by Savannah Morning News – Savannah Now.

5. "The Return of the British Army," www.georgiaencyclopedia.org/nge/Article.jsp?id=h-2709, The New Georgia Encyclopedia, History and Archaeology, Published by the Georgia Humanities Council, in partnership with the University of Georgia Press, the University System of Georgia/GALILEO, and the Office of the Governor.

6. *Holy Bible*, Revelations 12:3.

7. Amie Marie Wilson and Mandi Dale Johnson, *Image of America: Historic Bonaventure Cemetery Photographs and collections of the Georgia Historical Society,* Published by Arcadia Publishing.

8. Paige Williams, "Gullah: A Vanishing Culture," February 7, 1993; Published by the *Charlotte Observer*; Charlotte, N.C.; Page Number(s): 1A+.

9. Father Cliff Graham, "The Ritual of Exorcism," www.stmichael.pair.com/ritualofexorcism.html.

10. First Inaugural Address of Abraham Lincoln.

11. William C. Harris, *After the Emancipation Proclamation: Lincoln's Role in the Ending of Slavery,* Published by North & South vol. 5 no. 1 December 2001.

12. David D'Arcy and Ben Mammina, *Civil War Walking Tour of Savannah*, Published by Schiffer Publishing Ltd. Atglen, Pennsylvania.

13. www.savannahga.gov/cityweb/cemeteriesweb.nsf/f88b2a9 460d8675b8525704c006921d4/48e128575f599457852 5703500669825?OpenDocument, Published by the City of Savannah department of Cemeteries; Bonaventure Historical Society Inc.; P.O. Box 5954, Savannah, Georgia 31414.

14. Malcolm Bell, *Historic Savannah*, Published by the Historic Savannah Foundation, 1977, Tallahassee, Florida.

15. Murray Silver Jr, *One for the Road,* Published by Savannah CONNECT, February 8.

16. www.chicagohs.org/history/capone/cpn4.html; Published by the Chicago History Museum.

17. *Pirates and Buccaneers of the Atlantic Coast,* Edward Rowe Snow, Jeremy D'Entremont, Kenneth J. Kinkor.

18. *Pirates and Buccaneers of the Atlantic Coast*, Edward Rowe Snow, Jeremy D'Entremont, Kenneth J. Kinkor.

19. *Pirates and Buccaneers of the Atlantic Coast*, Edward Rowe Snow, Jeremy D'Entremont, Kenneth J. Kinkor.

20. www.ncmaritime.org/blackbeard/default.htm, Published by the North Carolina Maritime Museum, North Carolina Office of Archives and History, , 2002.

21. www.georgiaencyclopedia.org/nge/Article.jsp?id=h-466, Published by the New Georgia Encyclopedia, Land and resources, Sapelo Island.

22. "Slavery in Revolutionary Georgia," www.georgiaencyclopedia. org/nge/Article.jsp?id=h-2548.

23. Terry Matthews, "The Religion the Slaves Made," www.wfu. edu/~matthetl/south/nine.html, Wake Forest University.

24. *Holy Bible*, Eph. 6:5-6.

25. *Holy Bible*, Titus 2:9-10.

26. *Holy Bible*, 1Pet. 2:18-29.

27. *Holy Bible,* Matt. 24:45-46.

28. Jacqueline Tobin and Raymond G. Dobard, PhD, *The Heritage of an Oral Tradition: The Transmission of Secrets in African American Culture,* Published by Doubleday, New York, pages 1-2.

29. www.firstafricanbc.org, Published by The First African Church.

30. www.graveaddiction.com/wrightsq.html.

31. *Savannah Duels and Duelists; 1733-1877.* Published by The Reprint Company, Publishers; Spartanburg, South Carolina.

32. http://ngeorgia.com/ang/Button_Gwinnett, "About North Georgia."

33. Tom Coffey, *Only in Savannah*, Published by Frederic C. Beil, Savannah, Georgia, 1994, pages 156-157.

34. Tom Coffey, *Only in Savannah*, Published by Frederic C. Beil, Savannah, Georgia, 1994, pages 84-85.

35. Tom Coffey, *Only in Savannah*, Published by Frederic C. Beil, Savannah, Georgia, 1994, pages 168-170.

36. John Berendt, *Midnight in the Garden of Good and Evil*, Published by Vintage Books, a division of Random House Inc. New York, NY, Pages 60-64.

37. Cornelia Bailey and Christina Bledsoe, *God, Dr. Buzzard and the Bolito Man*, Published by Doubleday, New York, 2000, Pages 187-192.

38. Cornelia Bailey and Christina Bledsoe, *God, Dr. Buzzard and the Bolito Man*, Published by Doubleday, New York, 2000, Pages 140-142.

39. Edward Chan Sieg, *The Squares an Introduction to Savannah*, Published by The Donning Company/Publishers Norfolk, Virginia Beach, 1884.

40. tybeeconcierge.com/2008/03/16/savannah-squares.

Bibliography

Bailey, Cornelia and Christina Bledsoe. *God, Dr. Buzzard and the Bolito Man*, Published by Doubleday, New York, 2000.

Bell, Malcolm. *Historic Savannah*, Published by the Historic Savannah Foundation, 1977, Tallahassee, Florida.

Berendt, John. *Midnight in the Garden of Good and Evil*, Published by Vintage Books, a division of Random House Inc. New York.

"Biography of Tomo Chi Chi," www.tomochi-chi.org/History/history.htm, published by Savannah Online Now.

Coffey, Tom. *Only in Savannah*, Published by Frederic C. Beil, Savannah, Georgia, 1994.

D'Arcy, David and Ben Mammina. *Civil War Walking Tour of Savannah*, Published by Schiffer Publishing Ltd. Atglen, Pennsylvania.

Graham, Father Cliff. "The Ritual of Exorcism," www.stmichael.pair.com/ritualofexorcism.html.

Harris, William C. *After the Emancipation Proclamation: Lincoln's Role in the Ending of Slavery*, Published by *North & South* vol. 5 no. 1, December, 2001.

http://ngeorgia.com/ang/Button_Gwinnett, About North Georgia.

Lincoln, Abraham. *First Inaugural Address*.

Matthews, Terry. "The Religion the Slaves Made," www.wfu. edu/~matthetl/south/nine.html, Wake Forest University.

"Online Virtual Tour of Savannah–Wright Square," www. ourcoast.com/tours/savannah/wright.shtml , Published by Savannah Morning News – Savannah Now.

Piechoccinski, Elizabeth Carpenter. *The Old Burying Ground,*"*Colonial Park Cemetery, Savannah, Georgia 1750-1853*, Published by The Oglethorpe Press Inc., Savannah, 1999.

"Religion and the Founding of the Republic," www.loc.gov/ exhibits/religion/rel01.html, Published by the Library of Congress.

Savannah Duels and Duelists; 1733-1877, Published by The Reprint Company, Publishers; Spartanburg, South Carolina.

Sieg, Edward Chan. *The Squares an Introduction to Savannah*, Published by The Donning Company/Publishers Norfolk, Virginia Beach, 1884.

Silver Jr., Murray. *One for the Road*, Published by Savannah CONNECT, February 8.

"Slavery in Revolutionary Georgia," www. georgiaencyclopedia.org/nge/Article.jsp?id=h-2548.

Snow, Edward Rowe. *Pirates and Buccaneers of the Atlantic Coast*.

"The Return of the British Army," www.georgiaencyclopedia. org/nge/Article.jsp?id=h-2709, The New Georgia Encyclopedia, History and Archaeology, Published by the Georgia Humanities Council, in partnership with the University of Georgia Press, the University System of Georgia/GALILEO, and the Office of the Governor.

Tobin, Jacqueline and Raymond G. Dobard, PhD. *The Heritage of an Oral Tradition: The Transmission of Secrets in African American Culture*, Published by Doubleday, New York.

tybeeconcierge.com/2008/03/16/savannah-squares.

Williams, Paige. "Gullah: A Vanishing Culture," February 7, 1993; Published by *The Charlotte Observer*; Charlotte, North Carolina.

Wilson, Amie Marie and Mandi Dale Johnson. *Image of America: Historic Bonaventure Cemetery Photographs and collections of the Georgia Historical Society*, Published by Arcadia Publishing.

www.chicagohs.org/history/capone/cpn4.html; Published by the Chicago History Museum.

www.firstafricanbc.org, Published by The First African Church.

www.georgiaencyclopedia.org/nge/Article.jsp?id=h-466, Published by the New Georgia Encyclopedia, Land and resources, Sapelo Island.

www.graveaddiction.com/wrightsq.html.

www.ncmaritime.org/blackbeard/default.htm, Published by the North Carolina Maritime Museum, North Carolina Office of Archives and History, 2002.

www.savannahga.gov/cityweb/cemeteriesweb.nsf/f88 b2a9460d8675b8525704c006921d4/48e128575 f59945785257035006690825?. OpenDocument, Published by the City of Savannah department of Cemeteries; Bonaventure Historical Society Inc.; P.O. Box 5954, Savannah, Georgia.

Index